The Book of
Herb Spells

The Book of
Herb Spells

CHERALYN DARCEY

ROCKPOOL

For Pete Christie,
my brother in magick

How could such sweet and wholesome hours
Be reckoned but with herbs and flowers?
Andrew Marvel

A Rockpool book
PO Box 252
Summer Hill
NSW 2130
Australia

rockpoolpublishing.com
Follow us! f ⃝ rockpoolpublishing
Tag your images with #rockpoolpublishing

ISBN 978-1-925682-26-7
A catalogue record for this book is available from the National Library of Australia.

First published in 2018
Copyright Text © Cheralyn Darcey 2018
Copyright Design © Rockpool Publishing 2018

Cover design by Richard Crookes
Internal design and typesetting by Jessica Le, Rockpool Publishing
Printed and bound in China

10 9 8 7

The information presented in this book is intended for general inquiry, research and informational purposes only and should not be considered as a substitute or replacement for any trained medical advice, diagnosis, or treatment. All preparations and information about the usage of botanicals presented in this book are examples for educational purposes only. Always consult a registered herbalist before taking or using any preparations suggested in this book. No responsibility will be accepted for the application of the information in this book.

Contents

Welcome, Blossom

I welcome you to this *Book of Herb Spells*, no matter where you find yourself in your level of experience or interest with magick or herbs. The botanical world is my passion and I can not imagine a day without eagerly getting my hands dirty in my garden, being lost in an old botanical science text, or wandering about my local garden centre chatting with locals about plans for a coming season.

My love is sharing with you my enthusiasm for plants and nature, especially those of you who may feel they have two brown thumbs. Some of us may have an easy talent for gardening and plant-based work, but make no mistake: it is all skill-based practice and can be learned or, I believe, re-learned. There was a time we were all foragers and gardeners and our daily survival depended on our ability to live well in a relationship with the plants in our environment.

For as long as there have been people and plants, there has been a relationship between us. I strongly believe in co-evolution and the growth, through time, of plants' attributes in order to make them more appealing and beneficial to us, ensuring the survival of many botanical species. If a plant gives humans something they want or need, then humans will in turn replant it, tend it and care for it. No more strongly is this evident than in the plants we call herbs.

I would advise that you take time to develop your own relationship with herbs so you may strengthen your bonds with Nature Magick. If you do not have the space or the experience with gardening, or you have been unsuccessful in the past, I would love you to try again. Herb gardening is the very best place for anyone to begin, and for those of us who already dedicate ourselves to growing botanical treasures it is a place to find the sort of quiet corners one needs to uncover what we may have lost or may be seeking.

'Gardening with herbs, which is becoming increasingly popular, is indulged in by those who like a subtlety to their plants in preference to brilliance.'
HELEN MORGENTHAU FOX (1884–1974) – botanist, author and gardening lecturer

So what exactly are herbs? They are plants that, through their aromatic or savoury properties, present usage in medicinal, culinary or spiritual application. In this book of herbal spells, we will explore the magickal qualities of herbs and learn along the way the history and the botanical lore that will bring us again a little closer to Nature. In doing so we may instigate change, support, and inspiration when needed.

May Nature bless you always, but I hope that you too be the blessing that Nature needs!

Bunches of Blessings,

Cheralyn

Plate LXII.

῍ow to Use Ͳhis Book

It's never an easy task to create a book of instruction to suit everyone. What I prefer to do is to share with everyone the magickal ways one can work with herbs.

Those more experienced in spellcrafting and casting, or who have dedicated and defined paths in their own beliefs, may be able to skim the following instruction pages and dive straight into the spells, experimenting and exploring new paths which may open up, enhance or complement their work. Those who have a small amount, to no experience, in magickal work are cared for with information so that you may safely create and cast spells.

Though I suggest that everyone read through the first section in order to familiarise yourselves with the foundations on which I have presented this book of Nature Magick. For those who are complete beginners to having some experience, Section One will provide a good grounding in safe and best practice when creating and casting spells. This section also explains, in detail, what a spell is and how it works.

I have shared 60 spells that I have written over my life. They focus on herbs and their energies. They are arranged in smaller chapters by their use so that you can quickly find a spell that suits your needs. Make sure you observe the instructions I have given and any instructions you already use each time you are creating and casting spells.

All steps to using each spell are clearly explained, along with simple, everyday ingredients and tools to create them. I also share additional interesting and helpful tips with each spell to enrich your experience working with Nature, so you can get to know our herbs a little better.

At the end of this collection, I provide a special journal – a place to keep your own spells. In preparation for creating your own spells, I have included a simple guide to writing your own magick and then a collection of beautiful pages that you may use to keep your herb spells together with mine.

What if you don't have access to your own herbs?

As wonderful as it would be, to access every herb on earth, no matter where you found yourself, the reality is that you cannot. I have given you alternate herbs which you may be able to source and that hold similar energies, but I would also encourage you to dry your own herbs when they are available and create or source essences, candles, incenses and other botanical treasures from trusted suppliers so you have a magickal apothecary to always rely on.

What if you don't have herbs at all?

To further focus energy or to connect with herbs when you do not have access to them, imagery in the form of artwork, photos, your sketches or oracle cards can be used. I feel it is very important to see the herb to connect with its unique energy.

SECTION ONE
What Is a Spell and How Does It Work?

Calendula

What Is a Spell and How Does It Work?

A spell is a combination of ingredients, tools, actions and focus, which come together energetically to create change. Timings (when you cast your spell) can also be observed to ensure added power. These timings can be Moon or astrological phases, seasonal times and also correspondences that connect with days of the week or hours of the day or night.

✫ TIMINGS

I have included simple and broad timings in this book, which include Moon Phase, Day of the Week and Time of the Day. You can observe these to give your spell work a boost because working in line with the time of Nature is working in synchronicity with what is going on around you and provides stronger focus for your intentions.

Moon Phases
» *Waxing:* new projects, beginnings, growth
» *Full:* empowerment, healing, attainment
» *Waning:* banishing, cleansing, letting go
» *New:* divination, revelations

Day of the Week

» *Monday:* home, family, dreams, emotions, female energies, gardens, medicine, psychic development, travel
» *Tuesday:* courage, strength, politics, conflict, lust, endurance, competition, surgical procedures, sports, masculine energies
» *Wednesday:* communication, divination, self-improvement, teaching, inspiration, study, learning
» *Thursday:* luck, finances, legal matters, desires, honour, accomplishments, prosperity, material gain
» *Friday:* friendship, pleasure, art, music, social activities, comfort, sensuality, romance
» *Saturday:* life, protection, self-discipline, freedom, wisdom, goals, reincarnation
» *Sunday:* spirituality, power, healing, individuality, hope, healing, professional success, business

Time of the Day

» *Dawn:* beginnings, awakening, cleansing, new ideas, change, love
» *Morning:* growth, home, gardening, finances, harmony, generosity
» *Midday:* health, willpower physical energy, intellect
» *Afternoon:* communication, business, clarity
» *Dusk/Twilight:* reduction, change, receptiveness
» *Night:* pleasure, joy, socialising, gatherings, play
» *Midnight:* endings, release, recuperation

❧ INGREDIENTS

The ingredients you gather to create the spell will have correspondences to your intention. In a way, they illustrate what it is that you want to happen.

They will support the things you wish to happen because they have similar meanings and energies. These meanings and energies may also assist you in removing something. These correspondences are important because they also help us find substitute ingredients for our spells when what is prescribed is not available. I will give you my suggestions with each spell.

❧ TOOLS

Tools are additional items that you can use to help you create your spell. These are just a few examples of tools used in spellcrafting and casting:

» cloths to set your spell up on (*usually in colours which align with the energy of the spell*)
» wands and staffs to direct and enhance energies
» divination tools such as tarot and oracle cards, crystal balls, pendulums and runes to provide clarity
» drums and bells (*musical instruments and music express your intentions*)
» practical items such as glasses, cups, vases, bowls and cutting tools.

The way you put a spell together, the words you may recite, the things you actually do to cast your spell, are the actions that bring it all together. These focus your intention, put you squarely in the path of the outcome and strengthen the relationship between the energies of the ingredients and the tools you are using. The combination of all these things raises the energy for magick to happen.

❧ WHY WOULDN'T A SPELL WORK?

Not many things in life work all the time. External factors influence them; maybe they are not put together properly; sometimes it is just not meant to be. I'm sitting here writing my book for you on my laptop. I love my little computer, but it's rather clunky at times and has had its moments. It closes down for no apparent reason, loses files, can't be bothered accepting my Airdrops and decides I need to look at all the files with a certain keyword except the one I want. It appears to have a mind of its own.

You cannot change another person's free will and this is also why spells do not work at times. Perhaps the consequence of the spell will adversely affect another or counter their stronger will, which you might not even be aware of. Another reason a spell may not work is because other energies have greater strength at that moment or they may in fact be leading you to a better eventual outcome.

Spells work because the person creating and casting them fully believes in what they are doing and has a strong, focussed intention with a good connection to the energies of their spell and the outcome. While perhaps changing things for personal benefit, the outcome is still generally in keeping with a good outcome for all involved without forcibly changing anyone's free will.

ꙮ HOW TO CREATE AND CAST A SPELL

When you are using the spells in this book, please ensure you do so safely – and by this I don't just mean keeping burning candles attended to. Working with energies to create magick requires you to take responsibility for what you are doing, for yourself and the world you live in. There are many ways you can do this, just as there are many ways of life and beliefs with their own rituals, which ensure safety and power in spellcasting.

Most safety measures include a way to protect yourself and those around you. A way to mark the beginning of the spell or opening the space comes next. There will be words, meditation, music, chants or actions, which will help you focus on the task at hand, and then there will be a way to release the energy, perhaps give thanks and to close the space.

This is a simple and safe way to cast a spell.

Protect and Open

Before you can begin it's important to establish
protection from negative energies. There are various
ways you can achieve this, but whatever way you use
make sure you always protect yourself before casting.
You may wish to use a smudging method, by burning
sage or other plants, or by spraying the room with
a smudging mist. You can also visualise or draw a
circle around you and your spell with your finger in
the air, then fill your circle with white light.

If you are aligned with certain deities, elementals
or guides, you may wish to ask for their assistance
in providing protections. A very simple and effective
protection method is to light a white candle
while visualising the light cleansing, clearing and
protecting you.

Focus Intention

Sit or stand still for a long moment and imagine your
outcome. Really see it in your mind and complete
your picture with exact times, places and events. You
may like, at this time before you cast your spell, to
write down your intention and say it out loud to get
yourself fully focussed and your energy aligned with
what it is you are about to create.

Cast Spell

In each of the herb spells I have shared with you, I have set out very specific steps to create your spell and I have explained why I've used these steps. In the final section, I've provided instruction on creating your own spells. Casting your spell is simply what you do to make the spell happen. While casting your spell, you must maintain your focus on your intention.

Release, Close and Ground

Once you have completed your spell, you will need to release the power you have raised in creating it. I will provide a way to release the spell, for each spell I share with you, but you can also simply say: 'I release the power I have raised' or 'It is done' or by putting out your white candle if lit.

Grounding is the way you bring yourself back from your spellcasting time. Clapping your hands, ringing a bell or placing your bare feet or hands on the earth, are all ways to ground yourself.

❦ MAGICKAL CORRESPONDENCES

You may wish to create a bath, an essence, a tea, a mandala, in fact anything at all which will be in itself an action related to the energy of the spell. Items required for this should be aligned with your outcome. These are usually called Correspondences or Magickal Correspondences. I would suggest that to expand your knowledge in areas that you do not have experience with, you seek out resources that specialise in the item you are wishing to include such as Astrological, Crystal, Colour and so on. Following is a beginning list of such correspondences to get you started:

Colour

You can use colour in cloth, candles, flowers, additional ingredients and other tools, to set your spell upon.

- » *Red:* passion, power, strength, courage, renewal, health, motivation, self-esteem, confrontation, ambition, challenge, purchases
- » *Pink:* healing, calming, emotions, harmony, compassion, self-love, romance, relaxation, new beginnings, partnerships
- » *Orange:* opportunities, legal matters, obstacles, abundance, gain, power, happiness
- » *Yellow:* friendship, returns, productivity, creativity, education, healing
- » *Green:* wellness, new beginnings, marriage, home, planning, peace, harmony, birth, rebirth, fertility, affection, luck, change, creativity, socialising
- » *Blue:* self-improvement, opportunity, charity, study, growth, travel, insight, patience, meditation, sports, religion, social standing, expansion, higher education, wisdom
- » *Brown:* focus, lost items, grounding, harvest, security, generosity, endurance
- » *Violet:* psychic growth, divination, spiritual development, self-improvement
- » *Purple:* spirit, ambition, protection, healing, intuition, business, occultism
- » *White:* protection, safety, transformation, enlightenment, connection to higher self, becoming more outgoing, relieving shyness, the cycle of life, freedom, health, initiation
- » *Black:* divination, rebirth, material gain, discoveries, truth, sacrifice, protection, creation, death, karma, absorbing energies, binding, neutralisng, debts, separation.

Crystals

The addition of whole pieces of crystal, tumble stones, balls and jewellery can add specific energies to your spells. Not all crystals are suitable for all types of spells – some are not safe when they come in contact with items you use for consumption, or topically.

You will need to check the properties of the crystals before you create your spells. A reliable, specialised crystal-usage resource is advisable. Below is a basic summary of crystals and their properties:

» *Agate:* courage, longevity, love, protection, healing, self-confidence
» *Agate, Black:* success, courage
» *Agate, Black and White:* physical protection
» *Agate, Blue Lace:* peace, consciousness, trust, self-expression
» *Agate, Green Moss:* healing, longevity, gardening, harmony, abundance
» *Amazonite:* creativity, unity, success, thought process
» *Amber:* protection, luck, health, calming, humour, spell breaker, manifestation
» *Amethyst:* peace, love, protection, courage, happiness, psychic protection
» *Apache Tear:* protection from negative energies, grief, danger, forgiveness
» *Apatite:* control, communication, coordination
» *Aquamarine:* calm, strength, control, fears, tension relief, thought processes
» *Aventurine:* independence, money, career, sight, intellect, sport, leadership
» *Azurite:* divination, healing, illusions, communication, psychic development
» *Bloodstone:* healing, business, strength, power, legal matters, obstacles
» *Calcite:* purification, money, energy, spirituality, happiness
» *Carnelian:* courage, sexual energy, fear, sorrow release, action, motivation
» *Chalcedony:* emotions, honesty, optimism
» *Chrysocolla:* creativity, female energies, communication, wisdom
» *Citrine:* detox, abundance, regeneration, cleansing, clarity, initiative
» *Dioptase:* love attracter, prosperity, health, relaxation
» *Emerald:* wealth, protection, intellect, artistic talent, tranquility, memory
» *Epidote:* emotional healing, spirituality
» *Fluorite:* study, intellect, comprehension, balance, concentration

- » *Garnet:* protection, strength, movement, confidence, devotion
- » *Gold:* power, success, healing, purification, honour, masculine energy
- » *Hematite:* divination, common sense, grounding, reasoning, relationships
- » *Herkimer Diamond:* tension-soothing, sleep, rest, power-booster
- » *Iolite:* soul connection, visions, discord release
- » *Jade:* justice, wisdom, courage, modesty, charity, dreams, harmony
- » *Jasper:* healing, health, beauty, nurturing, travel
- » *Jet:* finances, anti-nightmares, divination, health, luck, calms fears
- » *Kunzite:* addiction, maturity, security, divinity
- » *Kyanite:* dreams, creativity, vocalisation, clarity, serenity, channelling
- » *Labradorite:* destiny, elements
- » *Lapis Lazuli:* love, fidelity, joy, healing, psychic development, inner truth
- » *Larimar:* confidence, depression, serenity, energy balance
- » *Malachite:* money, sleep, travel, protection, business
- » *Moldavite:* changes, transformation, life purpose
- » *Moonstone:* youth, habits, divination, love, protection, friends
- » *Obsidian:* grounding, production, peace, divination
- » *Onyx:* stress, grief, marriage, anti-nightmares, self-control
- » *Opal:* beauty, luck, power, money, astral projection
- » *Pearl:* faith, integrity, innocence, sincerity, luck, money, love
- » *Peridot:* wealth, stress, fear, guilt, personal growth, health
- » *Prehnite:* chakras, relationships
- » *Pyrite:* memory, focus, divination, luck
- » *Quartz, Clear:* protection, healing, power, psychic power
- » *Quartz, Rose:* love, peace, happiness, companionship
- » *Quartz, Smokey:* depression, negativity, tension, purification
- » *Rhodochrosite:* new love, peace, energy, mental powers, trauma-healing

- » *Ruby:* wealth, mental balance, joy, power, contentment, intuition
- » *Sapphire:* meditation, protection, power, love, money, wisdom, hope
- » *Sardonyx:* progression, finances, self-protection
- » *Selenite:* decisions, reconciliation, flexibility, clarity
- » *Silver:* stress, travel, invocation, dreams, peace, protection, energy
- » *Sodalite:* wisdom, prophetic dreams, dissipates confusion
- » *Sugilite:* physical healing, heart, wisdom, spirituality
- » *Sunstone:* sexual healing, energy, protection, health
- » *Tanzanite:* magick, insight, awareness
- » *Tiger's Eye:* courage, money, protection, divination, energy, luck
- » *Topaz:* love, money, sleep, prosperity, commitment, calm
- » *Tourmaline:* friendship, business, health, astral projection
- » *Tourmaline, Black:* grounding, protection,
- » *Tourmaline, Blue:* peace, stress relief, clear speech
- » *Tourmaline, Green:* success, creativity, goals, connection with nature
- » *Tourmaline, Pink:* friendship, love, creativity
- » *Tourmaline, Red:* projection, courage, energy
- » *Turquoise:* protection, communication, socialising, health, creative solutions

❧ HOW TO CREATE YOUR OWN HERB SPELLS

Your own herb spells can be incredibly powerful because they are so personal. Creating spells from herbs that have special meanings and memories to you, and ones which you feel strong affinity for, can enhance their energy incredibly.

After experiencing and practising some of the Herb Spells from my collection you may like to create your own based on the ways I have shown you, or to explore other practices. Just remember to be respectful, safe and focussed.

At the back of the book I have provided some completely blank journal pages so you can fill them in as you wish.

ꙮ HERBS FOR SPELLS

Tools and magickal ingredients can be obtained from bricks-and-mortar stores and online, but always be guided by your feelings when making purchases from these sellers. Make sure you feel comfortable and positive about these businesses because their energies will transfer.

Be aware that anything that comes into your space to use for spell work has no doubt passed through various other hands and should be magickally cleansed. I would do this by placing the items under running water, smudging with smoke or placing them underground in suitable wrapping or a container for a night.

As this is a book of herb spells, you will need to find a way to obtain the herbs. Of course the very best way would be to grow them. In the following chapter I will share some ideas and tips on how to do this, but I know it is not possible for everyone to garden, nor is it possible to grow everything in every place all the time.

I will indicate in which state (fresh or dried) the herbs can be used, but most spells I share in this book use dried herbs. Selecting fresh or dried herbs bound for magickal work should be done with as much care as you give to preparing the food you eat, if not more. Select herbs that look and feel energetically positive and make sure you take fresh herbs home swiftly and look after them. Remove excess foliage that may turn water brown. Use the excess immediately, or dry for later use. Snip stems at an angle to remove any dried ends and immediately place in water to enable them to take a good long fresh drink. Change water completely every two to three days and snip stems if the herbs appear to be drying or collapsing.

You can easily dry most herbs by tying in loose bundles and hanging in a cool, dry space. Single stems can also be dried on racks or pressed, and for those particularly dedicated there are various food dehydrators on the market that work very well. Another popular herb-drying method is the use of silica gel. Herbs are placed in containers layered with the gel in bead form and this dries out flowers over a number of weeks.

Once dry, keep your herbs in a cool, dry place, out of direct sunlight in airtight jars. Label by herb type. You may also like to add place, time or season in which the herb was harvested. Ensure that your herbs are completely dry before bottling or they will grow mold.

❧ HOW TO HARVEST HERBS

Correct plant identification is crucial as many plants are toxic and can even cause death. So while wildcrafting (harvesting plant material in the wild) is a wonderful way to collect your herbs, you must ensure that you have correctly identified the plants. There are many field guides on the market and I would insist that contacting local experts would be the safest option if you have no, or limited, experience.

The key to using plant material for spell work is in how you harvest the herbs, whether they are your own herbs or wild herbs. Do so with care and respect, never take more than half of any plant and never use iron metal in any of your harvesting tools as it will destroy the spirit of a herb. It is generally believed that herbs destined for medicinal and magickal work should be collected at sunrise or better still, during a New Moon. They are stronger from the energy of the Sun during sunrise and boosted by the New Moon phase.

Giving thanks to the herbs also ensures a balance of energies. This can be done with simple words or by giving something back in the way of an offering.

Traditionally this can be a copper coin, bread, sweets or cake, beer or grain.

❦ GROWING HERBS FOR MAGICKAL WORK

A garden, a magickal garden, can be anything from a vast estate to a pot plant. The most important thing is that you grow your herbs organically and with a positive intention. I try and use what I already have and love reusing old containers for pot plants. I'm also a very keen seed swapper and cutting collector.

To teach you how to garden is beyond the scope of this book but I would suggest that you seek out resources close to your home. Your local garden centre not only contains plants to purchase but people who know your area and what will grow there. They will also help you with any challenges you may encounter. Most can also order in plants for you – ones that may not be on display.

Local councils, land and environment bodies, and gardening clubs are all sources of local plant knowledge. The best people of all, however, are your gardening neighbours, who might provide good information about suppliers and other contacts.

When planting herbs, be sure that you are not growing anything that is considered an invasive weed in your area. Be very careful when considering herbs that may be toxic to others, especially wildlife or pets. Planning your garden is important, as is soil preparation, seasonal considerations and your climate zone. Below are a few resources to set you on your way to growing your own herbs.

Books

The Book of Herbs by Dorothy Hall
Yates Garden Guide 2017 by Yates

Herb Gardening by Beverly Hill

A Beginner's Guide to Herb Gardening by Dueep Jyot Singh and John Singh

Indoor Gardening by Will Cook

Small-Space Container Gardens by Fern Richardson

Websites

The Royal Horticultural Society (UK): www.rhs.org.uk

Gardening Australia: www.abc.net.au/gardening

National Gardening Association (USA): www.garden.org

Kew Gardens: www.kew.org

The Old Farmers Almanac: www.almanac.com

Moon Gardening Guide: www.moongardeningcalendar.com

Horticulture Week: www.hortweek.com

SECTION TWO

A Collection of Herb Spells

Calendula

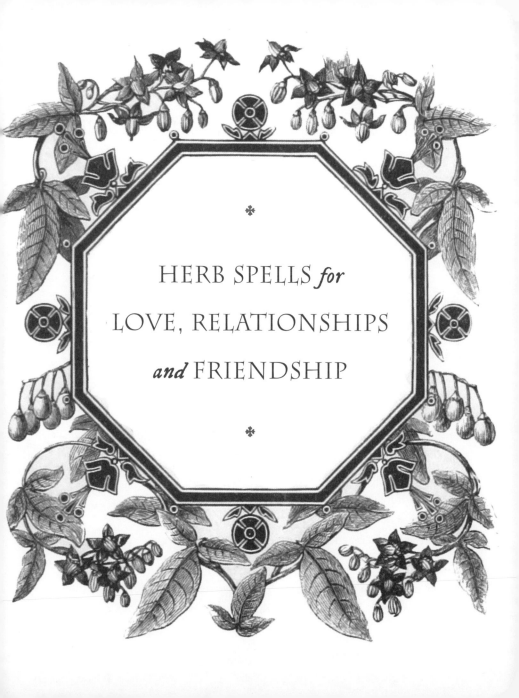

HERB SPELLS *for*

LOVE, RELATIONSHIPS

and FRIENDSHIP

Motherwort and Lemon Verbena Dispute Spell

Motherwort is included in this spell because it promotes trust, protection and motivation. This herb will ensure that everyone involved in a dispute is able to be open to a resolution or compromise. Lemon Verbena will help open the heart chakra of all those involved in the dispute. It will also lift negative behaviour patterns that may be getting in the way of constructive negotiations.

Timings

Waning Moon, Wednesday, Sunset

Find and Gather

- » ¼ cup of dried Motherwort (*Leonurus cardiaca*)
- » ¼ cup of dried Lemon Verbena (*Lippia citriodora*)
- » 4 drops of lemon essential oil
- » small rose quartz heart-shaped crystal
- » a beautiful bowl, preferably orange in colour
- » a piece of paper, pen and envelope

The Spell

You do not have to take notice of all the suggested timings for the additional energy boost, but you do need to ensure you create the spell on a morning and complete it by the following morning. Have all the items for the spell ready. Write down what your dispute is on the piece of paper and tuck it into an envelope.

Place the rose quartz heart-shaped crystal in your bowl and over it say:

Quietly now, be still and listen,

May everyone calm and now want a new mission.

Add your herbs and essential oil and mix well. Place bowl next to a window and put your envelope with your written dispute in it under the bowl. Note the time. Exactly 24 hours later take the envelope outside, burn it and say:

Dispute, you listened all day and night,

May you take our quarrels away with the light.

Resolution, welcome, here and now,

Let us all be open to knowing how.

Leave potpourri bowl where it is and top-up essential oil when you wish.

Alternate Herbs

Basil (*Ocimum basilicum*) can be used to substitute either or both herbs.

Culpepper, a revered 17th Century English herbalist, stated of Motherwort: 'There is no better herb to take melancholy from the heart.

In Morocco, Lemon Verbena is referred to as the friendship herb and is shared to celebrate and express all forms of friendship.

Slippery Elm Release-Anger Spell

Slippery Elm is derived from the inner bark of Red Elm, an American species of Elm tree. It is included in this spell for its ability to release anger and to soothe. An alternate herb, dried Vervain, can be used as a substitute. By adding almonds and Lavender flowers, additional cleansing and calming is imparted on your magickal powder.

Timings
Waning, Tuesday, Midday

Find and Gather
» 3 tablespoons of dried and crushed Slippery Elm (*Ulmus fulva*)
» 3 almonds
» 1 tablespoon of dried Lavender flowers (*Lavandula*)
» a yellow cotton bag
» a mortar and pestle

The Spell
Grind the almonds and Lavender together and then mix with the Slippery Elm.
As you do, say over and over:
Calm and calm,
soothe and soothe.
Place the mixture in your yellow bag and store.

Sprinkle it on the ground between you and the person who has, or is, displaying anger towards you. You can also sprinkle it across the threshold of your home to prevent angry energy entering your home.

To soothe the anger of a person, remotely, write their name on a sheet of paper, place it in a white cotton bag and sprinkle the spell powder into the bag. Shake and say:

Calm and Calm,

soothe and soothe.

May you see things more gently, wisely and cool.

Additionally, if you feel that anger is hard to let go of, sprinkle a circle on the ground outside around you in an anti-clockwise direction, and say:

Anger stay here, right in this spot.

Then hop out.

Alternate Herbs

Vervain (*Verbena officinalis*)

You can stop gossip directed at you by tying a length of yellow thread around a large piece of Slippery Elm and tossing it into a fire.

If a child wears a necklace created from the bark of the Slippery Elm tree they will grow up to be eloquent and even possess a very persuasive tongue.

Parsley and Mint Attraction Spell

Although Parsley is very entwined with folklore and historical usages as a herb associated with death, it is also very much a plant of attraction and celebration. The inclusion of Parsley in this spell will increase your powers of attraction and invite the energies of future celebration. Mint helps stimulate, and its addition will remove blocks between you and the one you desire, or towards a relationship you would like. The Rose bud will help add protection and courage, the rose quartz crystal another element of love as well as a boost in your ability to love and believe in yourself.

Timings

Waxing Moon, Friday, Morning

Find and Gather

» 1 tablespoon of dried Parsley (*Petroselinum crispum*)

» 1 tablespoon of dried Mint (*Mentha*)

» a tiny Red Rose bud

» a square of red cloth

» a rose quartz crystal

» a pink ribbon

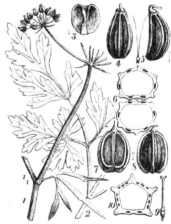

Fig. 475.

The Spell

Mix your Parsley and Mint, place in the middle of your red cloth and say:

Lift away the clouds, so others may see,

What is attractive and lovely in me.

Place the rose quartz crystal on the Parsley and Mint and say:

For love that is true

Place the Rose bud on the collection and say:

Unfurl and protect

Lift up the corners of the cloth and then twist to contain everything inside.

Tie with the pink ribbon.

Use when you feel you need to boost your attraction by tying to the tap over a bath so water runs over your magickal bath tea. Immerse yourself in the water and focus on your positive attributes. This bath helps bring these attributes to the fore.

Alternate Herbs

Parsley » Bay Leaf (*Laurus nobilis*)

Mint » Rosemary (*Rosmarinus officinalis*)

Mint is also associated with concentration and mental stimulation. Pliny the Elder (*AD 23 – 79*) a Roman author, naturalist and military commander, advised scholars to wear wreaths of mint to stimulate their minds.

It is believed that parsley needs to go down to the devil and back nine times before it can grow well, so you need to sow nine times more than what you actually need so the devil gets his share.

Comfrey and Dill Get-Closer Spell

This magickal, warm drink is an earthy, herbal honey water, which will be particularly good for those who feel they have drifted apart from one another. This could be because of a disagreement, but the spell will also be very effective for those who just want to take a relationship to the next level, or invite a warmer, closer bond. Comfrey is included for its power to bring energies together and to mend. Dill will enable people to see the attributes that attract them to another. Cinnamon will ease communication and, for those using this spell for romantic relationships, increase libido.

Timings
Waxing, Tuesday, Daytime

Find and Gather

» 1 fresh leaf of Comfrey (*Symphytum officinale*)
» 1 fresh sprig of Dill (*Anethum graveolens*)
» 1 tablespoon of organic honey
» 2 cinnamon sticks
» 2 cups of water
» 2 beautiful glasses

The Spell
Heat the Comfrey in a little water in a saucepan – about 2 cups of water to 1 leaf. Simmer for a few minutes, but do not boil. Remove from heat. Chop up the Dill, add to water and let cool a little. Use the water only in this spell

(you can always use the Comfrey as a compress for skin and bone healing). Place ½ tablespoon of honey into each of your glasses and say:

Sweet golden glow,
warm and heal.

Pour a tablespoon of the Comfrey-and-Dill water into each of the glasses and say:

Bring us together, Closer and close.

Top up the glasses with plain water.

Put a cinnamon stick in each glass and, holding one in each hand, stir in a clockwise direction. If you wish a friendship to be closer, say:

Bring us together, held fast in warmth,
Closer in friendship.

If you wish a romantic relationship to be closer, say:

Bring us together, held fast in warmth,
Closer in love.

Drink together. You may also wish to make a toast or express a commitment to each other.

Alternate Herbs

There are no alternates for this spell, but you can use 1 tablespoon of dried Dill and a very tiny pinch of dried Comfrey (*no more than a match head*) in place of fresh plants.

The name Comfrey (*Symphytum*) is derived from the Greek word symphyo, which means to make things grow together, to unite.

Placing a sprig of Dill and a pinch of salt in each shoe on your wedding day is said to ensure a good marraige.

Damiana and Cardamom New-Lover Spell

Cardamom has the ability to draw in a new lover and make you more attractive to others. Damiana is included because it is a powerful aphrodisiac and assists with psychic abilities, which can help sharpen your intuition and make you more alert to any opportunities that will help you find your new lover.

Timings
Full Moon, Friday, Evening

Find and Gather

- » 2 leaves or 2 pinches of dried Damiana (*Turnera aphrodisiaca*)
- » 2 pinches of Cardamom seeds (*Elettaria cardamomum*)
- » a mojo bag – a small red bag that you can carry with you
- » 2 dried Red Rose petals
- » a rose quartz crystal
- » a malachite crystal
- » a rhodonite crystal

The Spell
Hang your mojo bag outside your bedroom window before you go to bed and say:

Dance in the moonlight,

Sing in the air.

Welcome a lover,

Who is good, right and fair.

The next night place your Red Rose petals and Damiana leaves into the bag and place it under your pillow.

You may find you dream of your new lover or receive a message about how to meet them.

The next night add your malachite and say:

Let nothing from my past get in my way.

Add your rose quartz and rhodonite and say:

I welcome new love from this day.

Sprinkle the Cardamon into your mojo bag and close.

Wear it upon your person to attract a new lover.

Alternate Herbs

There are no alternatives for this spell.

Damiana is originally from Mexico and has been used as a powerful aphrodisiac in South American countries since the Mayan culture. It is also found in many modern herbal preparations for this use.

Chewing Cardamom seeds before going out in the evening will increase your sexuality and ensure you find a new lover, too!

Basil and Red Clover Fidelity Spell

Not only will Basil ensure the fidelity of a partner, it will protect against quarrels and even help mend those that have occurred. Red Clover will also ensure fidelity as well as lust between those who use it. Storing the mix over a few weeks will impart the energies of the Basil and Red Clover into the oil.

Timings
Full Moon, Friday, Evening

Find and Gather
» 4 fresh Basil leaves (*Ocimum basilicum*)
» 4 fresh Red Clover flowers (*Trifolium pretense*)
» sweet almond oil or coconut oil
» a beautiful airtight bottle that can hold at least 1 cup of oil

The Spell
Sterilise your bottle. This can be done by placing it in a pot of water and bringing it to the boil for five minutes.

Wash and dry the Basil leaves and Red Clover flowers completely.

Add both to your bottle and say:

Stay true to me with this flower and leaf.

Gently pour the oil into the bottle and say:

Hold all together,
Mix in the dark.
Next time you are open,
Release irresistible sparks.

Store for at least two weeks in a cool, dark, dry place.

To use, offer your partner a massage. Sprinkle the oil on them and massage lovingly.

If you are worried about being unfaithful, massage a little oil into your arms before going out or being in a situation in which you do not fully trust yourself, and say:

These arms will hold no other.

Massage onto your feet and say:

These feet will never walk away.

Alternate Herbs

Basil » no alternative.

Red Clover » Yerba Mate (*Ilex paraguariensis*) – use just a very small amount. A little pinch of dried Yerba Mate will work well.

In many European gardening folklores, you must curse the ground as you plant Basil, to ensure it grows well. This is because it is generally believed that this plant belongs to Satan.

Red Clover is used in many ways for purification. It makes a really good addition to smudge sticks. You can also add a flower to your purse or wallet to attract abundance and financial luck.

Meadowsweet Relationship-Ending Spell

Ending a relationship is never an easy task and so this spell is one that helps ease the transition period. This is a very good spell for those who wish to break up with someone, but it also supports those who have been told their relationship is over. You can use the butter each day on a simple piece of toast or treat yourself to something lovely like a muffin, scone or fruitcake slice. Meadowsweet will support you through the termination of the relationship and help you transition to a new chapter of your life and St. Mary's Thistle eliminates negative energies surrounding the breakup. You can use other edible substitutions for the butter, such as oils and vegetable spreads.

Timings
Waning Moon, Saturday, Midday

Find and Gather

» ¼ teaspoon of dried Meadowsweet
  (*Filipendula ulmaria*)
» ¼ teaspoon of dried St. Mary's Thistle
  (*Silybum marianum*)
» 1 cup of organic butter
» a small white ceramic bowl
» a wooden spoon
» a small wooden knife/spreader

The Spell

Beat the butter with the wooden spoon until it is fluffy, and say:

> *Light come in,*
>
> *Welcome and bright.*
>
> *Let a new day begin*

Sprinkle in the Meadowsweet and St. Mary's Thistle and say:

> *Herbs supportive,*
>
> *Join with me now.*

Keep this butter covered in the fridge.

Use for seven days straight. It is best eaten first thing each morning to ensure a smooth transition period after the breakup.

At the end of the seven days, bury whatever is left of the butter under a large and strong tree and say:

> *Take what is left.*
>
> *I am now free.*

Alternate Herbs

There are no alternatives for this spell.

Meadowsweet is one of the three herbs most sacred to the Druids and was used to flavour mead and wine. It contains Salicin, which is the ancient equivalent of aspirin, although meadowsweet is a much safer and natural pain reliever and anti-inflammatory and fever reducer.

Milk Thistle, also known as St. Mary's Thistle, has been used for centuries for liver ailments. It is believed that the milky marks on the leaves are the result of milk that fell from the breast of the Virgin Mary while she was breastfeeding Jesus.

Marjoram Communication Spell

Dedicate one plant solely for communication spells. Do not use the plant for any other purpose other than nourishment. Marjoram is used in this spell because it brings swift awareness to those in its presence or under its focus. It can bring people back into consciousness and, in fact, can be used for those who have fainted (in place of smelling salts). If you are unable to find a blue plant pot, purchase a plain terracotta one and paint it blue or tie a large blue ribbon around it.

Timings
Full Moon, Wednesday, Dusk

Find and Gather

» a small Marjoram plant (*Origanum majorana*)
» a portable yet good-sized blue plant pot
» good-quality potting mix
» a small chrysocolla crystal
» pure water

The Spell
Take your Marjoram plant, blue plant pot, potting mix and crystal to a very sunny spot outside. Half fill your pot with the potting mix and then place the chrysocolla crystal in the centre and say:

Crystal of communication, power and knowledge,

Open the paths.

Sprinkle a little water on the crystal.

Fill the rest of pot and then plant your Marjoram plant and say:

Magickal plant,

Open the way.

Let communication flow,

Each day and each way.

Take care of the plant in a way that suits your climate. You may need to grow it inside or in a particular spot in your garden. Seek local advice when you obtain your plant or find information in a gardening guide or on the internet.

When you need to improve the communication between you and another, simply position the plant near the place where you are expecting communication to come from. This could be the mailbox, your computer or your phone.

Alternate Herbs

Oregano (*Origanum vulgare*)

Marjoram was believed to have been created by the Greek goddess Aphrodite and so can strengthen love between two people. Young lovers in both Ancient Greece and Rome would wear wreaths of Marjoram on their heads to induce happiness and love.

The Ancient Romans believed that Marjoram grew on the graves of the departed who were happy in the afterlife.

Chicory Obstacle-Remover Spell

Chicory is considered the most powerful obstacle remover. You should dedicate this candle spell to just one person, institution or entity. Although there are a few ways to add dried flowers and botanicals to candles, I find the method below the easiest and most effective. Harvesting Chicory must be undertaken with additional energetic care. It is best to collect at either Midday or Midnight, and you must do so in complete silence.

Timings
Full Moon, Saturday, Midday

Find and Gather
» Chicory flowers and leaves (*Cichorium intybus*)
» a thick white pillar candle
» a tea light candle
» a metal spoon
» a heat-safe surface to work on
» a flower press
» a black cloth

The Spell
Chicory leaves are optional. You will first need to dry the Chicory flowers and leaves and you will need to use a method that ensures they are flat, so either use a flower press or an old book and tissue paper with weights.

Once the flowers and leaves are ready, set yourself up to create your candle by laying the candle on its side on the heat-safe surface.

Light the tea light and use this to heat the back of the metal spoon.

Place the first flower or leaf on the candle and lightly work the spoon over it so it presses down into the candle. The heat will transfer through the flower or leaf and melt the wax. Work gently and patiently.

As each flower or leaf is set, say:

*Our troubles pressed into wax *say the person's or thing's name*,*

Held softly there.

But I know the light will release into air.

Once the candle is decorated to your satisfaction, use it whenever you feel there are obstacles between you and the person or thing you created the candle for. Light it and watch the melting wax while envisioning the obstacles dissolving. When not in use, store the candle in the black cloth and only ever use it for this person or thing that you need to communicate with, and for this magickal purpose.

Alternate Herbs

Yarrow (*Achillea millefolium*)

Chicory is said to be capable of opening locks and can even expose people to various entrances to the Underworld.

Carrying Chicory will ensure good luck to travellers, especially those exploring new lands, seeking a new life, or even prospecting. It was a very popular herbal talisman during the North American gold rush.

Marshmallow and Chamomile Grief-Support Spell

Marshmallow is one of the great medical herbs and has been used extensively throughout history. The entire plant can be utilised and its addition to this spell takes advantage of its soothing properties. Marshmallow encourages good and supportive spiritual energies and banishes malevolent energies that can be attracted to us when we are in a low state of energy, which may be due to grief. Marshmallow was added to wine in Ancient Greek times to act as a cough suppressant as well as a soothing tonic. If you would rather create a non-alcoholic spell, I have included instructions on making this spell without the traditional wine. You will end up with the same results in a lovely tea.

Timings

Full Moon, Sunday, Midnight

Find and Gather

Althea Dioscoridis et Plinii, cap. 13...Althea Hortus, Rob Fuchsius... nec Malvaviscus ... 92. Gumm006 ordinaire

» 1 tablespoon of Marshmallow root
(*Althaea officinalis*)

» 1 tablespoon of dried Chamomile
(*Matricaria chamomilla*)

» 1 cup of white organic wine, or 1 cup of
pure water

» a screw-top glass jar

» a tea strainer

» a black glass or cup

The Spell

Gently warm the wine or water, without boiling. Pour into the glass jar.

Sprinkle Marshmallow root into the jar and say:

Energies soft and subtle relieve,

Calm and support this time that I grieve.

Sprinkle in the Chamomile and say again:

Energies soft and subtle relieve,

Calm and support this time that I grieve.

Swirl the mixture in a clockwise pattern and then place it in the fridge.

Sip as you will the next day. You can have it cool or you can warm slightly and sweeten with a little honey, if desired.

Alternate Herbs

There are no alternatives for this spell.

Marshmallow sweets, which today are created from a mixture of water, gelatin and sugar, were originally made from the roots of this plant, which has gelatinous properties. It was often used in cough drops.

Marshmallow bears the botanical name of Althaea officinalis. Plants which have the word officinalis in their name are recognised as being of importance, usually medicinally. Althaea comes from the Greek word 'altho', meaning 'to heal'.

HERB SPELLS

for HOME, FAMILY

and PETS

Skullcap and Oregano Settle Pet Spell

Historically, Skullcap has been used to remedy canine rabies. It is used in this spell as a calmative. Oregano helps bring awareness, and clarity and opens channels of communication, all vital when settling pets down after a difficult event that has caused them anxiety.

You will be creating a type of flower mist in this spell, and although the addition of glycerin will extend the mist's shelf life, I would suggest you keep it in the fridge.

Timings
Full Moon, Monday, Midday

Find and Gather

» a few Skullcap leaves (*Scutellaria lateriflora*)
» a few Oregano leaves (*Origanum*)
» some pure water
» a glass or crystal bowl
» glycerin
» a glass misting bottle

The Spell
Find a very sunny spot that will remain sunlit for at least an hour.

Place your glass/crystal bowl on the ground. Make sure it is on the earth or grass so that it becomes 'grounded'.

Half fill your glass/crystal bowl with the pure water, and say:

Water pure, ready to hold,

the energies of plants and their gifts from gold.

NOTE: 'gifts from gold' refers to this method of transferring the Sun's energy through the plants.

Gently place your Skullcap leaves upon the water and say:

For *say your pet/s name/s*.

Settling herb, your gifts to share.

Then place the Oregano upon the water gently and say:

For *say your pet/s name/s*.

Clarity herb, your gifts to share.

Leave your bowl out in the full sun for an hour. Take the herbs out and bury them, with thanks, under a large, healthy tree. Bottle the water in misting bottles: 4 parts water to 1 part glycerin. Spray around the areas your pet/s live in. The mist can also be sprayed, sparingly, directly on pets.

Alternate Herbs

Oregano » Marjoram (*Origanum majorana*)

A North American native, Skullcap's botanical name (*lateriflora*) describes the interesting way the flowers and seedpods only grow on one side of the stem.

Native Americans called the plant 'Mad Dog' due to its reputation for curing rabies.

Hop Neighbour-Boundary Spell

The inclusion of Hops in this spell instills the energy of peace. Although there are Hops in the beer you will be using, more are needed to secure the boundary of your home or neighbourhood. Black tourmaline crystal will offer protection from negativity, as will the length of black ribbon. Although this spell will make friendships between neighbours easier, it will protect your privacy as well, making you and your life appear uninteresting to others, unless you step forward. It will also make neighbours with negative energy want to move on.

Timings
Waning Moon, Wednesday, Evening

Find and Gather

» a large cup of dried Hops (*Humulus lupulus*)
» a bottle of hop-based organic, home or craft-brewed beer
» a clear glass/crystal dish/plate/bowl
» 2 long black tourmaline crystals
» a length of black ribbon (*approximately 70 cm/27.5" long*)
» a blank invitation card
» a pen

The Spell

Define an area between you and the neighbours and focus on this area. This could be near your fence line that your neighbours look over or through, a wall that you can hear them through, or the front door if they constantly visit, unwelcomed.

Tie a black tourmaline crystal to each end of the black ribbon and lay it on the ground or floor at your defined point, as a barrier between you and your neighbours.

Fill in the invitation with your neighbour's name and yours.

If you do not know their name/s, then describe them.

For the 'event', write: 'To share this space in peace'.

Set the invitation down on your side of the ribbon.

Place the dish on the ground on their side of the ribbon and place the beer, opened, in the centre. Sprinkle the Hops onto the dish, around the beer, and pick up the invitation, prop it up in front of the beer on their side of the ribbon, and say:

I invite you to now share this space in peace,

Let what has occurred before now cease.

Leave in place for at least an hour and, if possible, bury the invitation, Hops, ribbon and crystal in this place. Pour the beer over the top. If not possible to bury then place all items in a box (except the beer) and keep as close as possible to your boundary with them.

Alternate Herbs

You could leave out the additional Hops. There are no alternates for this spell.

For those suffering insomnia, you can make a very effective sleep pillow by loosely stuffing a small cushion or bag with dried female Hop flowers and Lavender.

Not always favoured as an ingredient in beer, Hops was actually banned from use by some authorities in England in the 1530s due to its inferior taste and quality.

Ginkgo, Lavender and Sage Family-Blessing Spell

A blessing box can be used in a variety of ways; this one is created with herbs, intentions and magick, and is opened to release blessings when a family is in need of additional support. Wishes, prayers, rituals and offerings can be made over and to the blessing box.

Ginkgo is included in this spell because it facilitates flow and because it has remained fairly unchanged since prehistoric times. The plant can live for over 1,000 years and is said to hold the energy of life – perhaps even 'The Tree of Life' itself. Lavender is included for its calming, protective and cleansing energies and Sage for its wisdom, protection and negativity-clearing abilities.

Timings
Full Moon, Monday, Sunrise

Find and Gather
» ¼ cup of dried Ginkgo (*Ginkgo biloba*)
» ¼ cup of dried Lavender (*Lavandula*)
» ¼ cup of dried Sage (*Salvia officinalis*)
» a small wooden box with a lid
» a photo/s of your family
» paper, pens and pencils
» a white tablecloth

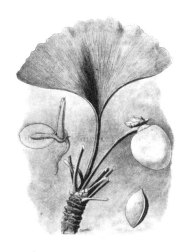

The Spell

Gather all family members to sit down at a table, if possible. Lay the white tablecloth out on the table and place the wooden box in the centre. Give each person pens, pencils and paper. Ask them to draw something that makes them feel happy. If any family member is distant or unable to do this, then you can do it for them.

Place the dried herbs into the box and say:

Plants of protection,

love and of earth,

Live now together

and blessings impart.

Put your photo/s in the box.

Add the drawings one by one and say each time:

A blessing of happiness upon us.

Store the box somewhere central in your home. The blessings and magick will always be imparted on you all, but in times of additional need open the box and say a prayer, make a wish, blessing or place a request over it. When you do, be sure to thank the box with a little additional sprinkling of any of the herbs.

Alternate Herbs

There are no alternates for this spell.

Women who comb their hair while seated beneath a male Ginkgo tree will have their wishes granted.

To ensure Sage grows well, someone else must buy it or give it to you, and you must plant it.

Echinacea and Bay Home-Protection Spell

This little bag will provide protection for your home while you are away. It can be used continuously in a special place, but for an added boost when you wish to go away for an extended period you should give your mojo bag a little energetic boost by repeating the chant below, over it, and adding a little more Echinacea. Make sure you thank your bag when you return from longer trips. Echinacea will protect your home and draw good energies to it, especially if needed for a particular reason. For example, if there is a natural disaster in your area, your mojo bag can attract support to protect your home. Bay leaves are always a good addition to spells when you are looking to stop outside influences or negative actions.

Timings
Full Moon, Monday, Midday

Find and Gather

- » 1 tablespoon of dried Echinacea leaves/ flowers (*Echinacea purpurea*)
- » 3 dried Bay leaves (*Laurus nobilis*)
- » small black bag
- » a teaspoon of salt
- » black ribbon (*30 cm/12"*)
- » a black obsidian crystal

The Spell

Place the obsidian into the black bag, and say:

Protect this home from within and without.

Absorb and dispel energies of doubt.

Sprinkle in the salt, and say:

Protect and ground,

Within and without.

Put the Echinacea into bag, and say:

Protect and hold,

Within and without.

Add the three Bay leaves, and say:

Together you three,

No one cross over.

Decide where it is you wish to keep your mojo bag. The best place is the most central area in your home, preferably hung from the ceiling with the black ribbon. For an energetic boost, plait the ribbon first.

Alternate Herbs

Cloves (*Syzygium aromaticum*), Basil (*Ocimum basilicum*), Sage (*Salvia officinalis*)

Echinacea, which originated in North America, is used by the Native American Plains Nations, in healing, more than any other plant.

Bay Laurel is thought by many cultures throughout history to be one of the strongest protective plants, especially when used in the home. Burning the leaves has traditionally been part of exorcisms.

Chive Garden-Guardian Spell

This spell allows you to dedicate a rock as your Garden Guardian, if you do not currently have one. Chives are used for their powerful energy offering protection, in general, but particularly against disease. Chives boost the vitality of the space around them and those within it. Plant your Chives next to a rock that you decide will be your Garden Guardian and use the chives to create your blessings and protection oil now, and again in the future.

Timings
Full Moon, Monday, Morning

Find and Gather
» a seedling plant of Chives (*Allium schoenoprasum*)
» olive oil
» a glass bottle with stopper
» pen and paper

The Spell
You will need to dedicate a particular rock as your Garden Guardian. This can be a magnificent standing stone already in place, or one you move there yourself, or it can simply be a smaller stone, even tiny, that you dedicate. The size is not important, it is the energy, intention, love and care with which you regard this rock.

Once such a rock is identified, set aside a good hour to dedicate yourself to your rock. Sit with it, in a sunny place in your garden, and write down on the pen and paper all that you wish for in your garden. Include your hopes, the things you wish to do with the produce, what you hope to gain, learn and share with this space. Fold the paper twice and bury it deep next to your rock. Next, plant your chive seedling onto the paper, and say:

Protector of rock,

Live here now.

Pick three chive leaves and place them into the glass bottle. Fill with olive oil.

Leave in the sunshine, next to the chive plants and rock, for an hour.

You may wish to use the oil to anoint your Garden Guardian.

Simply trickle a little of the oil on your fingers and then rub them on the rock while saying something special to mark the occasion. As an example:

Awake my Garden Guardian.

Watch over all who live and grow here

With love, guidance and protection.

Use your Garden Guardian oil in tiny amounts to add additional protection around plants, boundaries, on tools, and even on yourself, for protection and blessings of good fortune.

Alternate Herbs

Garlic (*Allium sativum*), Leek (*Allium ampeloprasum*)

To give your Chives a boost, feed them your coffee grounds. They add much-needed minerals to ensure good growth.

Chives come to us from Asia, where they have long been prized as a respiratory illness remedy. They are also known to chase away evil energies, especially those energies ready to prey on the sick.

Garlic House-and-Contents Selling Spell

*Garlic helps with breakthroughs and so it is perfect for anyone trying to sell –
anything! – but is particularly good for people who sell online from home. It can
even be used for selling the house itself! Rosemary is used to protect your financial
transaction and to ensure the value of the item you are selling is appreciated. Gold is
the colour of abundance, so you are going to use it liberally.*

Timings

Waxing Moon, Thursday, Daytime

Plate CIV.

Find and Gather

» a clove of Garlic (*Allium sativum*)

» a sprig of rosemary

» a white pillar candle

» 4 gold coins

» a gold permanent marker

» a gold candleholder/plate

» a compass

The Spell

Place your golden candle onto your holder/plate.

Sprinkle rosemary leaves onto it, and say:

Today I begin a spell to sell.

Today I will find a buyer.

They will love the item I have to sell,
in fact it is all they desire.

With your gold pen, draw the object you want to sell on your candle. Cut the garlic clove in half and rub it over your candle holder/plate. Place the candle in the middle of the sprinkled Rosemary leaves on the plate and place it in a window that faces the street, or close to the main entrance to your home. Place the gold coins around the candle at North, South, East and West. Use the compass to be sure if you do not know North. When you are ready to invite the selling energy, light the candle and say:

From all directions,
Let them come.
Buy my *say whatever it is you are wanting to sell*
Before the setting of the Sun.

The time that you do this could be during the 'open for inspection,' if selling a house, or when you have someone negotiating the sale of an item with you either in person or via the phone or even via email. You can cut the flame and relight it at any time (this boosts the energy). But leave it in your window/near your front entrance until you sell your item.

Alternate Herbs
There are no alternates for this spell.

Rosemary has been used as a magickal ingredient, usually a wash, to promote longevity and beauty, for centuries. It ensures that people, and objects, are appealing.

Garlic has been used in healing for well over 3,000 years. Ancient Egyptians revered it so much and they believed that onions and garlic were equally powerful and deities, themselves, that could be called upon when making oaths.

Passionflower Sweet-Family Spell

Passionflower will not only bring balance to a situation and between people, it will calm everyone down. This spell is very effective between sparring siblings and could be called a school-holiday magick potion.

Timings
Waning Moon, Wednesday, Dusk

Find and Gather

» 1 tablespoon of dried Passionflower (*Passiflora incarnata*)
» 1 cup of fresh lemon juice
» ¾ cup of castor/fine sugar
» 1 cup of boiling water
» 2 cups of cold water
» ⅓ cup of additional water
» a large glass jug to store lemonade in fridge

The Spell
Mix together the boiling water and the sugar and stir until dissolved. Let cool completely.

Bring to the boil the Passionflower and ⅓ cup additional water. Remove from heat and let cool completely.

Add lemon juice and cold water to the sugar mix and say:

Sweet and sour,

Mix and mingle.

Add the Passionflower mix and say:

Balanced and calm,

Waters flow.

Bring happier times,

Wherever you go.

Store in the fridge and serve in tumblers full of ice cubes.

This drink is particularly good to serve if siblings are not getting on or they are about to go on a trip together or share an activity.

Alternate Herbs

You can use commercially prepared organic Passionflower tea.

NOTE: Passionflower should only be consumed in small amounts and occasionally.

Passionflower is a mild sedative and is used extensively in herbal remedies for insomnia, anxiety and stress.

Christian missionaries in Spain during the 15th Century integrated the flowers of Passionflower within their teachings: the ten petals represent the ten apostles; the radial filaments represent the crown of thorns; the three stigmata, three nails; the five anthers, five wounds; the tendrils, the whips used against Christ; and the blue and white colours represent Heaven and purity.

Feverfew and Comfrey Travel Spell

This talisman can be easily slipped into a cotton crochet crystal holder or tiny mojo bag. You might like to craft a loop out of air-dry clay to thread a necklace chain or cord through. You can also tuck the talisman into your bag or suitcase. Walnut shells are perfect natural lockets as they are natural guardians of magick.

The addition of Feverfew will offer you protection from accidents and Comfrey will ensure safe and trouble-free travels. The crystal malachite is used in this spell for its ability to offer protection to travellers, to ward off the 'evil eye' and for the additional gift of helping those who fear flying.

Timings
Full Moon, Thursday, Midday

Find and Gather

» ¼ teaspoon of dried Feverfew
  (*Tanacetum parthenium*)
» ¼ teaspoon of dried Comfrey
  (*Symphytum officinale*)
» two clean and dry walnut shell halves
» a very small malachite crystal
» strong glue
» optional: crochet crystal holder or tiny
  mojo bag

The Spell

Mix together the Feverfew and Comfrey and place into one half of a walnut shell.

Place the malachite crystal on top of herb mix and say:

Travel well,

Within this shell.

Take me with you,

Travel well.

Glue the two walnut shells together and leave to dry as per the glue manufacturer's instructions.

You may like to decorate the closed walnut shells or cover them in air-dry clay.

Wear when travelling.

You can give this talisman to another, but ensure that you ask their permission to cast a spell over it for their protection.

Alternate Herbs

There are no alternates for this spell.

In many Italian fairytales, walnuts are depicted as containing something very precious.

Feverfew has been used to protect against accidents and as a medicinal aid for the injured. During the construction of the Greek Parthenon in 5 BC, a workman's life was saved after being treated with Feverfew. Such was the regard for the incident that the plant still today bears reference to it with the name parthenium.

Lemongrass and White Sage Argument-Release Spell

The use of smoke in magickal work assists in spreading the energies you wish to impart into a space and also releasing those you do not want, which the smoke takes away when it dissipates. For this reason, it is vitally important that you open all windows and doors when wanting to release certain energies. This helps them waft away with the smoke.

The addition of Lemongrass in this spell helps improve communication and refresh the atmosphere, which will probably be rather heavy after a disagreement. Sage is a favourite for smudging because it offers protection and very effectively clears away negative energies.

Timings

Waning Moon, Wednesday, Evening

Find and Gather

- » a small bunch of Lemongrass leaves (*Cymbopogon*)
- » a small bunch of Sage leaves (*Salvia officinalis*)
- » organic cotton or hemp string
- » a feather or firm leaf
- » a bowl
- » sand

The Spell

Bunch together your Lemongrass and Sage leaves. Ensure that they are dry (not fully dried, though). Cut a piece of string at least four times the length of your bundle.

Tie your bundle together very tightly at one end, at the top of the leaves.

Wind your string to the end of the bundle in a spiral type pattern. Tie off at the end and cut off the string. Tie the string again at the bottom and wind the string up the bundle but this time try and crisscross across the previous string. You should end up with the bundle firmly held together with the string.

As you are winding the string, say:

Around I circle you, around and within.
The blessings you share with me.
The blessings I send.

Hang to dry out completely for a few weeks in a cool, dry place.

To use, ensure that all windows and doors are open. Light the end (with the leaves) with a flame. Once it has caught, gently blow out so it is left smouldering. Use the feather or leaf to help waft the smoke around the space you wish to cleanse and empower. Put out embers on your smudge stick by pushing it into sand-filled bowl.

Alternate Herbs

Lavender (*Lavandula*), Cedar (*Cedrus*)

Growing Lemongrass around the garden is said to keep snakes away from your home.

Write a wish on a Sage leaf and place it under your pillow for three consecutive nights. If you dream of what you wish for, you will receive it. If you do not, then make sure you bury the leaf in the garden. To not do so can cause bad luck.

Gotu Kola Dog-Training Spell

Liquid Gotu Kola drops are relatively easy to obtain from health-food shops, but should you be lucky enough to have access to the plant, simply boil up a cup of water and a handful of leaves, strain and use ¼ cup of the liquid in this recipe.

Gotu Kola helps with memory and to ensure the mind stays focussed, but most importantly it imparts calm. This spell is best done when giving your dog a bath, but you can also place the Gotu Kola into a misting bottle and top up with water and spray lightly over your dog's coat before a training session.

Timings
Waxing Moon, Wednesday, Midday

Find and Gather

- » 10 drops of liquid Gotu Kola (*Centella asiatica*)
- » 4 cups of pure water
- » 1 cup of baby shampoo
- » 1 cup of apple cider vinegar
- » 1/3 cup of glycerin
- » large glass bowl
- » wooden spoon
- » glass bottle to store

The Spell

Place all the ingredients together into the glass bowl.

Slowly stir in a clockwise direction to mix well, and say:

Magickal mix, created with care.

Calming and learning the things that we share.

You may also like to add a few drops of Lavender essential oil for fragrance. Lavender will also impart an additional calming influence should your dog be highly excitable.

The addition of 2 tablespoons of pure Aloe Vera gel will assist dogs who may have sensitive skin or be experiencing heat rash or any other mild skin irritation.

Pour into a glass bottle, seal and keep in a cool, dry place.

To use, shake well and use about a tablespoon for a medium-sized short-haired dog. Adjust the quantity to suit the size and coat of your dog. Lather up well and, as you do, speak calmly to your dog about training and your hopes and goals for it, which you will both benefit from.

Rinse your dog very well.

Alternate Herbs

Brahmi (*Bacopa monnieri*), Rosemary (*Rosmarinus officinalis*)

Gotu Kola is also known as Pennywort and has been used for hundreds of years for many health issues including arthritis and other age-related problems. A popular saying testifies to this: 'Two leaves a day keeps old age away.'

A traditional Sri Lankan breakfast dish, 'Kola kanda', is created from Gotu Kola, boiled rice and coconut.

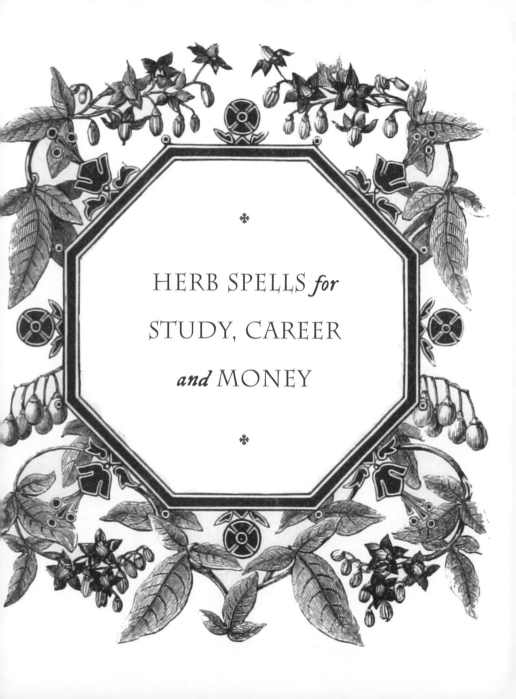

HERB SPELLS *for*

STUDY, CAREER

and MONEY

Hawthorn Work-Harmony Spell

Hawthorn imparts harmony, happiness and fertility. It makes a very good herb to use in workplace spells, ensuring that everyone is working productively, getting on and being happy.

You should obtain permission before tapping into anything in their personal space and I have given suggestions for alternative places to position your spell boxes.

The option of black tourmaline could be considered if there have been very stressful/ negative workplace dramas — it will clear the energy and offer support against the negativity returning.

Timings
Full Moon, Wednesday, Sunrise

Find and Gather

» dried leaves/flowers of Hawthorn (*Crataegus laevigata*)
» a small matchbox for each work station or desk
» strong tape
» optional: a tiny piece of black tourmaline for each box

The Spell

Place all matchboxes in a circle.

Add a small pinch of hawthorn into each box, working in a clockwise direction, and say with each:

Harmony, happiness, working together.

Happiness, harmony, no matter the weather.

If you would like to add an additional energetic boost, particularly if there is a lot of tension in the workplace, add a tiny piece of black tourmaline.

Tape a box under each desk/workstation. As you do, say:

Harmony, happiness, working together.

Happiness, harmony, no matter the weather.

If obtaining permission for those you work with is not possible, you can either bury a box at each corner of your workplace building or tape one in each inner corner of the workplace.

If tensions rise in the office, try tapping three times gently on your box and say:

Calmly now,

Settle low.

Work together as we go.

Alternate Herbs

Hops (*humulus lupulus*)

Hawthorn, Oak and Ash trees growing together indicate places where you may see faeries.

Maypoles are often created from, and decorated with, Hawthorn branches. Because Hawthorn symbolises fertility, love and marriage, it is a good choice for May Day fertility-connected rites and rituals.

Thyme New-Place Spell

The addition of Thyme in this spell helps to make the wearer of the oil more attractive to others, but it also gives the wearer courage and a boost in energy. This support can help when settling into a new job, a new place of study or even undertaking a new pastime, hobby or sport.

Only a very small amount needs to be used, but still, make sure that you use carrier oil that suits your skin. Roll or place a drop on your inner wrist when needed. Empty roller bottles can be sourced online. You can use a small dropper bottle as well.

Timings
Waxing Moon, Sunday, Sunrise

Find and Gather

» 11 fresh Thyme leaves (*Thymus vulgaris*)
» sweet almond oil or other skin-safe pure oil
» a glass/crystal bowl
» a gold cloth
» a picture of the place of your new beginning
» a small glass roller bottle or dropper bottle

The Spell
Set this spell up in a sunny place – one you feel really safe and happy in because you want this energy to blend with the oil.

Lay down the gold cloth and set the bowl upon it.

Pour the oil into the bowl.

Place the 11 Thyme leaves into the bowl and say:

Starting now,

With things all anew.

Thyme guide me there

With the things that you do.

Leave the bowl in the sun for a good hour to absorb the positive energies of your chosen place as well as the power of the Sun.

After an hour, stir the Thyme-infused oil in a clockwise direction and then pour into your bottle and seal.

To use, roll or drop a tiny amount on your inner wrist or your inner arm and rub in.

Use before you go to your new place and any time you feel uneasy and can no longer detect the scent of Thyme.

Alternate Herbs

There are no alternatives for this spell.

Thyme will help you see fairies. Wearing it in your hair, in a locket or pinned to your clothing will allow you vision into their world.

A popular herb with the Ancient Greeks, Thyme was used to purify sacred places such as temples as well as being burnt for magickal rituals. You could do the same today.

Catnip Change-at-Work Spell

With its mint-like and refreshing properties, Catnip will help invigorate any situation. Apply after washing and conditioning your hair, especially on the first day of your working week, to see energies move in your favour. Catnip also attracts happiness and friendship. An added benefit of this rinse is that it promotes a healthy scalp, and removes dandruff and build-up of residue.

Don't make this rinse too far ahead; it should be created no more than 24 hours before you wish to use it. The perfect time would be the night before the first day of your working week.

Timings
Full Moon, Late Night

Find and Gather
» 2 tablespoons of Catnip leaves (*Nepeta cataria*)
» 2 cups of pure water
» a glass jar

The Spell
Boil the water and then remove from the heat.

Add the Catnip and stir well.

Cover and leave for a few hours to steep and cool, then strain into a glass jar or other glass container.

Wash your hair as usual and then pour the Catnip rinse over your hair. Massage through hair and focus on exactly how your day will look when your changes happen. Be very specific.

Say the things you want to occur, out loud.

Then rinse out.

Don't use this rinse too often if you have dry hair as it can be a little harsh.

The effects will last a very long time so you really do not need to, anyway.

Alternate Herbs

There are no alternatives for this spell.

Shake hands with a person you wish to be long-time friends with while holding a catnip leaf. Keep the leaf somewhere safe and the bond will last forever.

Catnip is entwined strongly with magick, possibly because cats, which are a Witch's familiar, love this herb. It is said that if you provide it for your cat, a strong psychic bond will develop between you both. A dried larger leaf is believed to be the very best bookmark for any magickal texts.

Goldenseal New-Skills Spell

Awaken yourself to being receptive to learning new skills with the properties of Goldenseal. As well as bringing a calm and cooling effect, this herb helps open up the magickal energies of possibility. Herbalists often use Goldenseal in conjunction with other herbs to boost their effectiveness. For this spell you will need something connected with your new skill. This can be a textbook, a tool or other materials.

Timings
Waxing Moon, Wednesday, Late Night

Find and Gather
» 1 tablespoon of dried Goldenseal (*Hydrastis canadensis*)
» 1 cup of pure water
» a fluorite crystal bracelet, pendant or tumblestone
» a glass/crystal bowl
» something connected with your new skill
» a piece of paper (*larger than your bowl*)
» a pen
» an orange cloth

The Spell

Bring the water to the boil and add the Goldenseal.

Simmer for a few minutes, then take off the heat and let cool completely.

Place your paper on a table and put the bowl upon it. Set up the thing you selected to represent your new skills above your bowl (above means the side furthest from you on the opposite side of the bowl to you).

Pour the Goldenseal water into the bowl.

Take your fluorite crystal and lower it into the water and say:

Sealed with gold,
New skills be mine.

Using the pen, write down all the things you will need to learn in order to gain your skill. Don't worry if you cannot think of all of them. Write as many as you can and then say:

May I learn all that I need
to be all that I want to be.

Take out your fluorite and dry it on the orange cloth. Wear or carry it with you when you undertake study or training for your new skill. Fold the paper and bury it under a large tree. Pour Goldenseal water over it.

Alternate Herbs

Ginkgo (*Ginkgo biloba*)

Goldenseal was an important medicine for the North American Indians. It was used for a vast amount of ailments and as an antibiotic and antiseptic.

You can also use Goldenseal in spells to promote abundance and to increase your finances.

Allspice and Patchouli Luck Spell

Patchouli is included in this spell because it helps things to grow and attracts money. Allspice is a naturally lucky herb and is also a good friend of money. The use of a citrine crystal will help with prosperity. Aventurine is also included because it supports those seeking luck.

Timings
Full Moon, Thursday, Morning

Find and Gather

» ½ cup of dried Allspice (*Pimenta dioica*)
» ½ cup of dried Patchouli (*Pogostemon cablin*)
» 2 green candles
» a beautiful box with a lid
» a green cloth
» a citrine crystal
» an aventurine crystal

The Spell
Place a green candle in a holder on either side of your box
    Place the green cloth into the box
    Add the citrine crystal and say:
    Brilliant crystal,

Glow and my luck grow.

Place the aventurine crystal in the box and say:

Lucky crystal,

Share your charms my way.

Sprinkle in the Allspice and say:

Herb of Earth,

Herb of Money and Luck,

Grow.

Sprinkle in the Patchouli and say:

Herb of Earth,

Herb of Money and Abundance,

Grow.

Light the candles and leave them until they burn out. Place the candle stubs inside the box. When you wish to boost your luck, open the box and ask for it.

Alternate Herbs

Patchouli » Bergamot (*Citrus bergamia*)

Allspice » Basil (*Ocimum basilicum*)

Sprinkling Patchouli into your purse or wallet will attract money. Sprinkling Patchouli directly onto the money you plan to use for investment or gambling is supposed to add luck.

Allspice is made from the dried, unripe berries of a Pimenta tree.

Ginseng and Guarana Study Spell

Ginseng has been used for centuries in herbal medicine and magick to increase and maintain stamina as well as cure just about anything. Guarana is a natural stimulant, which contains caffeine, but also other compounds, which seem to prolong its effect. The inclusion of Ginseng and Guarana in this spell harnesses those attributes to create a small mojo bag that you can carry on your person to give you a mental and physical boost while studying.

Timings
Waxing Moon, Wednesday, Late Night

Find and Gather

- » 1 teaspoon of dried Ginseng (*Panax pseudoginseng*)
- » 1 teaspoon of dried Guarana (*Paullinia cupana*)
- » a small gold bag
- » a tiny piece of paper
- » a pen
- » a tiny magnifying glass or piece of glass with smooth edges

The Spell

Place all the ingredients for your spell before you.

Take your piece of paper and write the following words on it:

Study hard and study well.

Focus strong and focus well.

Place the tiny magnifying glass or piece of glass on the centre of the paper. Fold the paper up around the glass, then pop the bundle into the gold bag.

Sprinkle the Ginseng into the bag and say:

All that I need is provided.

All that I need to do I can.

Sprinkle in the Guarana and say:

Study long, study well.

Close the bag and carry it with you whenever you are studying.

Alternate Herbs

None are suitable, though you can create this spell with just one of the herbs. Be mindful that although either is good for study, you will miss the additional attributes each brings.

The Latin name of Ginseng affirms its reputation as a cure-all. 'Panax' is broken down to 'pan', which means 'all', and 'ax', which comes to us via the word 'akos', meaning remedy. Ginseng has been in use in China for over 5,000 years.

Guarana is an Amazonian plant, which has been used for centuries by local Amazonian cultures. Most myths about the herb relate to its appearance – the peeled seeds that look very much like human eyes. All myths seem to tell of an unfortunate incident and the gods gifting the Guarana to the tribe to somehow make things right.

Elecampane Legal-Success Spell

Elecampane is used in this spell because it has a very strong influence on progress and so can help you move legal matters along and to your favour. Bay leaves bring victory.

Timings

Full Moon, Thursday, Morning

Find and Gather

» dried or fresh Elecampane flowers (*Inula helenium*)

» 1 Bay leaf (*Laurus nobilis*)

» an orange cloth

» an orange candle

» a knife, scalpel, awl or something to carve candle with

The Spell

Lay out the orange cloth.

Carve the candle with the date that is important to your legal matter. This should probably be the court or arbitration date.

With both hands, hold the candle before you and say:

*On *say the date* my time will come.*

say the outcome you desire

Will be done.

Place the candle in a holder in the middle of the orange cloth.

Beginning at another corner of the cloth, first place the Bay leaf, pointing to the left then place your Elecampane flowers in a row which gradually spirals around the candle until you circle around and around and end up at the candle. You can intersperse the spiral with small white flowers if you have not found enough Elecampane flowers.

Once you reach the candle, light it and say:

We meet at the middle,

Balance shall be.

Now light my way forward,

A win for me.

Once the candle has burnt down, bury the flowers and candle stub in the earth. If your legal matter involves you wanting to receive something, then bury on your property. Should a win mean that you are released from something, then you must bury as far away from your property as you can manage.

Alternate Herbs

If you do not have many Elecampane flowers, you can fill out your spiral mandala with simple white flowers such as Daisies.

The flowers of Elecampane often smell like chocolate and the roots, when dried, of sweet Violet. The plant is used to flavour absinthe along with other liqueurs, beers and confectionery.

Elecampane was a very treasured medicinal herb in monasteries throughout Europe. Its properties for healing respiratory diseases are well documented, particularly for whooping cough (*when all else has failed*).

Wild Yam and Potato Money Spell

Wild Yam is native to North America and is included in this spell because it has properties that attract abundance. Potatoes ensure prosperity and comfort, and the action of planting this spell encourages growth. Be sure that you look after your 'Money Plant' well.

Timings
Waxing Moon, Thursday, Daytime

Find and Gather

» 1 tablespoon of dried Wild Yam root (*Dioscorea Villosa*)

» a gold coin

» a large potato

» a patch of sunny earth (*from the garden*)

» a knife

» a spoon

» a length of gold ribbon (*30 cm/12"*)

The Spell
Cut the potato in half and, using the spoon, scoop out a hole in one half, big enough to fit your gold coin and Wild Yam root into.

Place your coin into the hole and say:

Seed of gold,

Time to grow.

Sprinkle Wild Yam root onto the gold coin and say:

Fertilised and fed,

Awake from your bed.

Put the potato back together and tie gold ribbon around it to hold the halves together.

Bury near the front entrance of your home, in a sunny spot, preferably on your land.

Water and care for your Money Garden as you would any garden.

Water, weed and watch over it.

You may like to decorate the area. If you are having money problems in the future, fertilise again by sprinkling Wild Yam root over the earth.

Alternate Herbs

There are no alternatives for this spell.

Wild Yam was also known as Devil's Bone and can be used for other magickal purposes including carrying a piece in a red cloth so one might attract a suitable new lover.

Soak Wild Yam in rainwater overnight and then use it to wash your hands before performing magickal work. It will increase your power.

Valerian Make-the-Best-of-Things Spell

Valerian is used in this spell because it helps us to accept the way things are but to still make the best of them. It is also a herb for protection and purification, which may support you when you find life a little difficult.
Kyanite crystal is said to boost our determination and stimulate creativity.

Timings

Waxing Moon, Saturday, Daytime

Find and Gather

» a small chunk of Valerian root
» a teaspoon of dried, chopped Valerian root (*Valeriana officinalis*)
» a small dome-type hand-rung bell
» a small square of white cloth
» a tiny Kyanite crystal
» some string

Plate XLVIII.

Valerian. (*Valeriana officinalis.*)

The Spell

Take the ringer out of the bell.

Place the chopped or crushed Valerian root into the middle of the small piece of cloth and place the Kyanite crystal in the centre.

Tie it into a ball to replicate a bell ringer. You might need to trim excess fabric.

Tie a piece of string to the original anchor point inside the bell and then the ball of Valerian root to the other end of the string. It may hang a little lower than the original ringer

Keep the bell in a sunlit spot, preferably a windowsill so it can absorb the positive and optimistic energies of the Sun each day.

When things are not going your way and you are looking to make the best of your situation or to encourage ideas and inspiration to find your way forward, 'ring' the bell three times and say:

May I find that I can do as I please,
With what I've been given.

Alternate Herbs

Frankincense (*Boswellia*)

The Pied Pier used a piece of Valerian root as well as a flute to encourage the rats of Hamelin to leave. It was this myth that lead rat poison manufacturers to include it in their formulas.

The Ancient Greeks would hang Valerian under their windows to ensure evil would not enter the house.

Sandalwood and Cinnamon Better-Business Spell

Sandalwood inspires and keeps optimism fresh. Cinnamon is a herb that attracts luck in business, as well as money. In this spell you will be leaving the 'dreamcatcher-like' circle completely open so you may catch more business. Using ribbons, threads and yarns in red, yellow and orange will encourage success, creativity, and boost workers' and customers' passion for your business.

You can make this catcher as large or small (even very tiny) as you desire. It will not affect the power of the spell.

Timings
Waxing Moon, Thursday, Daytime

Find and Gather
» pieces of dried Sandalwood (*Santalum*)
» pieces of dried Cinnamon (*Cinnamomum verum*)
» wire or a wire coat hanger
» wire cutters
» pliers
» scissors
» strong electrical tape
» ribbons, threads and yarns in various shades of red, yellow and orange

The Spell

Cut a length of wire from your coat hanger or cut the wire you have to the desired length (enough to create a circle large or small enough to your liking).

Bring the two ends together and connect by overlapping the ends of the wire and twisting them together with the pliers. Then cover the join with the electrical tape.

Tie your collection of ribbons, yarns and threads to the bottom 1/3 of the circle so that they hang down from the circle. Make them random lengths and mix them up.

Next, tie pieces of Cinnamon and Sandalwood to some of the hanging ribbons.

Make sure you end up with an even number of pieces of the two herbs.

Once you have completed your catcher, hang it in a place that faces the door to your business, or if you have a home/online business, hang it facing either the front door or your main working area and visualise your business increasing and becoming very successful, and say:

Welcome, business,
Old and new.
Let's grow together,
Me and you.

Alternate Herbs

You can create this circle by using just one of the herbs.

The fragrance of sandalwood comes from its heartwood. The tree was recognised as having been saved from extinction after Tippu, Sultan of Mysore, India, declared it a 'Royal Tree' in 1792.

Cinnamon is native to Sri Lanka and southern India. Cinnamon oil was used by the Ancient Egyptians in their embalming process.

H. Webber inv.ᵗ   T. Holloway sculp.ᵗ

HERB SPELLS *for*

PROTECTION,

CLEARING

and BANISHMENT

Agrimony and Coltsfoot Bad-Vibe Clearing Spell

Agrimony has a long history of being a very good home protector. It is also a general protective herb against evil. Coltsfoot is included in this spell because it has the ability to cleanse an area and add tranquility in its wake. It is a spreading plant, much like mint, and it is this as well as the other mentioned qualities that make it a great floor-wash herb. Orange Blossom water will effectively and positively lift the energy.

Timings
Waning Moon, Monday, Late Night/
Midnight

Find and Gather

» ½ cup of dried Agrimony (*Agrimonia eupatoria*)
» ½ cup of dried Coltsfoot (*Tussilago farfara*)
» ¼ cup of Orange Blossom water
» ½ bucket water

The Spell
Open all the windows and doors of the space you wish to cleanse of bad vibes.

Mix together all the ingredients in a clean bucket.

Place the mop in and mix in a clockwise direction, and say:
Herbs of happiness,

Herbs of light,
Dark vibes now leave,
Good vibes in sight.

Wash over the floor and, as you do, visualise the bad and negative vibes leaving via the doors and windows while the good vibes are welcomed in. Pour the remaining water into the ground under a good, big tree.

Alternate Herbs

You can substitute the Orange Blossom water for Rose water. Coltsfoot can be a little difficult to obtain, so a good substitute is Lavender (*Lavandula*).

Agrimony has a solid reputation for being a multi-faceted healer of nearly all human adverse conditions. Its name suggests it has benefits to eye problems – 'agremone' means 'white spec on the cornea'.

Coltsfoot is used to create a UK confectionery product named Coltsfoot Rock. It is from Lancashire, England and is a hardened stick of brittle rock candy flavoured with Coltsfoot.

Tansy and Mugwort Protection Spell

A Seguro, created by South American Sharmans, is a magickal bottle filled with herbs. Seguros are believed to hold the shadow side of the Sharman and the spirit of the herbs. Shaking the bottle awakens the magickal energy. In this Seguro spell, we are harnessing the energy of the Sun and the Moon to create a powerful guardian. Tansy is added to represent the Sun and offer you longevity and life, while Mugwort is there to represent the Moon and will gift you strength and protection.

Timings
Full Moon, Wednesday, Dusk

Find and Gather
» 1 tablespoon of dried Tansy (*Tanacetum vulgare*)
» 1 tablespoon of dried Mugwort (*Artemisia vulgaris*)
» a beautiful bottle with seal/lid
» pure water
» 1 teaspoon of tiny pebbles or crystals

The Spell
Put the Tansy and Mugwort into your bottle and say:
> *Herb of Sun,*
> *Herb of Moon,*

Together watch over me
Day and Night.

Put the pebbles or crystals into your bottle and say:

Grounded in Earth
The Spirits hold true.

Top up the bottle with water.

Blow into the bottle three times and then quickly seal.

Blowing into the bottle adds your energy to the Seguro and the spirits of the herbs so that they will know you, to take care of you and protect you.

Place your Seguro where you feel you need protection.

If you need additional help, shake the Seguro bottle three times and simply ask for its help.

Alternate Herbs

Tansy » St John's Wort (*Hypericum perforatum*)

Tansy is thought to prolong life. This belief is said to have come from the story of Ganymede, who was given Tansy so he could become immortal. Ganymede was a Trojan prince, who was turned into an eagle and then carried off to Heaven by the god Zeus, where he became the cup-bearer of the Gods.

Folklore states that if you put Mugwort into your shoes you will be able to walk all day. Roman Soldiers did this so they could march for prolonged periods.

Yerba Mate Barrier-Breaker Spell

Yerba Mate is a stimulant and will assist you in breaking through any obstacles you are currently facing. It will activate things that have been dormant or have not been working. There are many spells that prescribe freezing objects in order to hold their energy, but in this spell we are meeting the 'frozen' barrier and then bursting through it.

Timings
Waxing Moon, Tuesday, Midday

Find and Gather

» about a teaspoon of Yerba Mate (*Ilex paraguariensis*) in any form
» a piece of paper
» a pen
» a ziplock bag or similar
» pure water
» a hammer
» a thick towel

The Spell
Write your obstacle on the piece of paper.

Put the paper in the ziplock bag.

Half-fill the ziplock bag with the water.

Place the Yerba Mate into the bag and seal.

Shake well to mix.

Put in the freezer and leave for seven days.

Each morning take out the bag, breath over it and say:

Slowly you melt, walls soon to fall.

Soon to be down and I'll have it all.

On the seventh day, take the bag outside.

Place it on the towel and smash up the ice as much as possible.

You must be thinking of your obstacle as you do this.

Visualise the obstacle disappearing with the ice.

Collect all the remains of the spell and bury far from your property.

Alternate Herbs

Agrimony (*Agrimonia*)

Yerba Mate is a traditional South American herb used for medicines and in ritual. It is said to have been gifted to the tribes by a 'white-bearded God'.

The stimulating effect of Yerba Mate makes it a milder and, some think, healthier alternate to coffee because it does not interfere with sleep.

Foxglove and Dragon's Blood Complete-Protection Spell

The creation of witches bottles goes back hundreds of years and, still today, occasional bottles from years ago have been dug up. Witch bottles were popular throughout the UK and Europe and even North America. They were traditionally buried in the front garden of a home to protect the house, garden and all who lived within.

You will need a selection of sharp objects for this spell. These can include: pins, needles, broken glass, broken mirror, razor blades, metal pieces, nails and thorns. Foxglove is included for its powers to protect the home – especially the gardens and borders of properties. Dragon's Blood is a resin obtained from the trees of the Dracaena family of plants and it is included here for its exceptionally good reputation for providing protection, and exorcising demonic and evil entities.

Timings
New Moon, Saturday, Midnight

Find and Gather
» 1 teaspoon of Dragon's Blood resin (*Dracaena*)
» 9 fresh or dried Foxglove flowers (*Digitalis*)
» a selection of sharp objects
» a glass bottle with a lid
» urine or vinegar

» 1 tablespoon of coarse-ground salt

» a candle

» newspapers

The Spell

Fill the bottle to about half way with all the dry ingredients and then add the urine or vinegar until the dry ingredients are covered.

Secure the lid and then seal it with wax. To do this, hold bottle on its side over a newspaper, light the candle and drip wax over the bottle's lid until it is fully covered.

Bury the bottle approximately 12 inches deep in your front yard.

The protection will last a year and you should create a new witch bottle each year. You do not need to dig up the old bottles, nor should you.

Alternate Herbs

Traditionally, all Witches Bottles are made with urine, but white vinegar is a good substitute.

If you add a tiny pinch of Dragon's Blood resin to any other incense, you will increase its potency. This is also true for herbs in spells. If you feel you need a magickal boost, try a tiny sprinkle.

In Wales, a dye was made from Foxglove and painted on the floors of homes, in crossed lines, to stop evil from entering.

Juniper Berry Personal-Boundary Spell

Sometimes it can be very hard to set personal boundaries. If you are feeling that yours are not being respected or that setting them is a challenge, then this spell will help you focus good and clear energy to not only set boundaries but keep them strong. Juniper will provide personal protection from accidents, sickness and negative spiritual activity like malevolent ghosts, and break any magickal work directed towards you.

Timings
Full Moon, Sunday, Dusk

Find and Gather

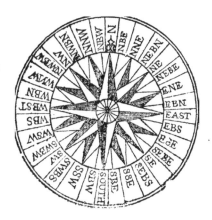

- » a dozen dried Juniper berries (*Juniperus communis*)
- » a large sheet of paper
- » a pen/pencil
- » a white candle
- » 4 black candles
- » a heatproof dish/incense burner
- » a block of incense/charcoal
- » matches

The Spell
Draw a compass on your paper like the one pictured here.

Place a black candle next to each of the Cardinal Points: North, South, East and West. Light the candles and say:

Power of light from the dark,

Hold my space and protect.

Place three Juniper berries between each candle on the curve of the compass.

Place the white candle in the middle of the compass. Light it and say:

Filled with purity,

Filled with light.

Let the candles burn down (almost to their ends) and then light the incense/charcoal as per the manufacturer's directions. Place the incense/charcoal in the heatproof dish/ incense burner and drop the Juniper berries into it. The smoke will further purify and strengthen your personal boundaries.

Bury all remains of your spell under a tree on your property.

Alternate Herbs

Rose Geranium flowers (*Pelargonium graveolens*) can be used in place of the Juniper berries. If you wish to burn these flowers you will need to dry them first and then crush them.

It is believed, particularly in Wales in the United Kingdom, that anyone cutting down a Juniper tree will bring death to themselves or to a family member within a year.

In the Scottish Highlands, the New Year has been marked with the burning of Juniper incense to ensure good fortune for the coming year.

Garlic Psychic-Attack Protection Spell

Garlic is one of the most powerful protectors against evil, negativity and misfortune. In this spell, you will be weaving strands of hemp or cotton with dried garlic leaves to make a simple bracelet that is very effective in stopping psychic attack or intrusion. People are often unaware that they are intruding upon others with their psychic energy. This is very common at larger gatherings. You may wish to weave some crystal beads or light charms into your bracelet.

Timings
Full Moon, Sunday, Late Night

Find and Gather
» dried stem of Garlic (*Allium sativum*)
» hemp or thick cotton string
» a black candle
» a white cloth
» a black cloth
» a bowl of water
» 9 drops of Lavender essential oil (*Lavandula*)
» a thick hand towel

The Spell
Select a quiet corner of your home or garden to create this spell. Smudge the area well with your choice of an energy-clearing and protecting smudge. You

could also use a Lavender or Sage misting spray. Drop the Lavender essential oil into the bowl of water. Soak the hand towel in the water and then wring out and lie flat. Separate a long but thin piece of garlic stem and wrap in the washcloth. This will help it absorb the Lavender oil and also soften it to make it easier to work with. Set out your white cloth with all of your ingredients for this spell, then cover with the black cloth and say:

Quietly rest, Pure in dark.

Nothing to find.

Leave for one hour.

When you return, take off the black cloth, light the black candle and say three times:

Dark light, fill the night.

Take the garlic stem and the hemp or cotton string and create a simple plait to a length that will fit your wrist. Tie off each end with a knot. Extinguish the candle flame once you have finished. This bracelet works better if used for only one occasion, event or trip. After use, bury in a place far from your home.

Alternate Herbs

Larger dried Society Garlic leaves (*Tulbaghia violacea*)

Garlic has been used since ancient times to ward off evil. The Sanskrit name of Garlic, lasunam, means 'slayer of monsters'.

Garlic harvested on Good Friday is said to hold the strongest medicinal qualities.

Angelica and Honeysuckle Release, Ground and Balance Spell

Using the root of one plant and the flower of another will bring balance and power by combining what is above with what is below. This spell requires the two halves of an eggshell. I recommend that you use the egg white and yolk to ensure that new opportunities know that you will not waste them.

Angelica will offer protection and guard over the balance of your energy, while Honeysuckle will inspire generosity, luck and peacefulness as well as dispel negativity.

Timings

Full Moon, Saturday, Dusk

Find and Gather

» a small piece of Angelica root (*Angelica archangelica*)
» 3 fresh or dried Honeysuckle flowers (*Lonicera*)
» an egg
» a piece of paper
» a pen
» clear tape
» pure water

Angelica.

The Spell

Dig a hole big enough to bury your eggshell in the ground in a dark area on your property.

Crack your egg and retain egg white and yolk for another use. Be very careful and try to crack your egg so that you have two halves.

Write your hopes on the piece of paper.

Place your Angelica, Honeysuckle and your written hopes into one half of your shell and then close it as best as you can with the other half, sealing together with clear tape.

Bury your magickal egg in the hole you dug.

For the next seven nights sprinkle a little water on it and say:

Grow my hopes, little flowers,
From above and below.
May balance return to all that I know.

Alternate Herbs

This spell could still work with a combination of a root and flower from any two plants.

Angelica is named after the Archangel Michael and is said to have been his gift to humans as a cure of the plague. Its seeds were often chewed as a form of protection against all contagious diseases.

The root of Angelica is a very popular talisman with the Native Americans when carried on the person. It is believed to promote luck, particularly when gambling.

Nettle and Meadowsweet Reverse Negative-Action Spell

This spell salt can be used in a variety of ways, including a bath salt and as an addition to other spells. You can sprinkle it in a circle around you to contain the negativity you may have caused and then hop out of the circle, or you could add the salt to a water misting bottle and spray an object or place which has caused, or is connected with, negative action.

Nettle is very good at reversing actions, from curses to bad luck, and can help reverse any negative actions you may have made or those you experience around you. Meadowsweet will help bring peace to all those connected with the action and lift spirits in order to feel positive about moving on from the negativity.

Timings
Waning Moon, Saturday, Dusk

Find and Gather
» 2 tablespoons of dried Nettle leaves
   (*Urtica dioica*)
» 2 tablespoons of dried Meadowsweet
   (*Filipendula ulmaria*)
» 1 cup of rock salt
» a mortar and pestle
» a glass storage jar

The Spell

Place the rock salt, Nettle and Meadowsweet into the mortar and grind together well. While you grind move the pestle in an anti-clockwise direction – this is a spell in which you want to put the energy of 'undoing' something into.

You need the mix to be fairly fine. When you are happy with the mix, turn the bowl three times anti-clockwise and say with each turn:

All that was done,

Turn around and undo.

Unravel, go back,

All that was done.

Store the dry ingredients in the glass jar and use as required.

Alternate Herbs

None are suitable for this spell, although the Meadowsweet could be substituted with Meadowsweet flower essence.

Nettle is considered a 'Plant Doctor' and can ensure the good health of all other plants growing near it. Nettle is also believed to have been brought to Earth, from Heaven, by the Angel of Mercy.

If you would like to see fairies and chat with them, inhale fresh Meadowsweet flowers. Doing so gives you the gift of second sight.

Fennel and Cloves Paranormal-Banishment Spell

In this spell you will be making a pair of maracas from two very powerful banishing herbs, Fennel and Cloves. Shaking these herbs will send all types of unwanted paranormal entities out of the area you are cleansing. Rhythmic sounds have been used throughout time in this way, to clear energies and to welcome new ones in.
Fennel will offer healing, protection and purification to your spell while Cloves will offer their own form of protection and, if necessary, will help exorcise any entities found. You may wish to decorate your maracas. Doing so will lift the energy and help expel unwanted paranormal activity.

Timings
Waning Moon, Tuesday, Midnight

Find and Gather
» 2 tablespoons of Fennel seeds (*Foeniculum vulgare*)
» 2 tablespoons of Cloves (*Syzygium aromaticum*)
» uncooked rice
» 2 cardboard tubes
» an A4 sheet of sturdy cardboard (*you can recycle 2 x used mailing tube with caps for the previous 2 items*)
» a marker
» packing tape
» decorative paints and embellishments

The Spell

Decorate your cardboard tubes or A4 cardboard sheet as you like. You may wish to be a little more creative and paint a design. Stand your cardboard tubes upright on your A4 cardboard sheet and trace out two circles for each tube. These will serve as the ends of your maracas. Cut all circles out and with packing tape seal one circle to one end of each of your cardboard tubes. Now fill your tube with 1 tablespoon of Fennel seeds and 1 tablespoon of Cloves and enough rice to fill the tube to about a third. Seal the tube with the other circle and packing tape.

To use, simply shake both maracas in a rhythmic way around areas you feel are experiencing unwanted paranormal activity. The maracas can also be used in combination with other methods and spellcastings focussed on banishment of paranormal acitivity.

Alternate Herbs

One of the herbs can be omitted as they have similar energies. Double the quantity if you need to do this.

Fennel was commonly used on Midsummer's Eve in Medieval times to protect against enchantment.

Cloves are very good at masking odours, which is probably why, in folklore, they have a reputation of making those who carry them on their person more attractive to the opposite sex.

Hyssop and Honey Purification Spell

It is good practice to set aside teacups that are dedicated to singular magickal purposes. In this spell, for example, the purpose is purification and so a white teacup is best. The cup could feature a white flower or design, which will not only attract energies associated with the particular colour and design but also remind us not to use it for any other purpose.

Timings
Full Moon, Sunday, Evening or
Morning

Find and Gather
» dried Hyssop (*Hyssopus officinalis*)
» organic Honey
» pure water, preferably Full Moon rainwater
» a beautiful teapot
» a white, or predominantly white, teacup
» a white candle
» a white cloth
» a tray

The Spell
Use 1 teaspoon of Hyssop to each cup of boiling water in your teapot.
    Sweeten tea with honey. Sit quietly somewhere in the sunlight to drink

your tea.

Create a purification ritual to surround the occasion. Here is one which you may enjoy:

Set a tray with a white cloth, and say:

Covered in purity

Set the candle in a holder on the tray, light it and say:

Filled with light

Place the teapot, teacup/s and honey pot and spoons on the tray and take to where you will be drinking the tea. You might like to add a White Rose and perhaps a clear quartz crystal to the setting.

Raise the cup before the first sip, and say:

Fill me with good, with light and with love.

Leave me/us anew with blessings from above.

Alternate Herbs

There are no alternatives for this spell.

Hyssop has been used since ancient times as a strewing herb, to purify temples and homes; branches of Hyssop were dipped in blood to paint doorways at Jewish Passover.

The liqueur Chartreuse is one of many liqueurs flavoured with Hyssop – the herb was very popular in European monasteries where brewing experiments with many medicinal and sacred herbs were conducted.

HERB SPELLS *for*

HEALTH, SELF-CARE

and HAPPINESS

Ginger and Peppermint Creativity-Boost Spell

Smelling salts have been used for centuries to revive one who has fainted. In this spell you will be creating a magickal mix to revive and boost dormant or sluggish creativity. This spell is perfect for writer's and artist's block and includes Ginger, to stir passion, and Peppermint, for its ability to raise energetic vibrations.

This smelling-salt mixture can be added to a tiny bottle to be carried and opened when needed, or you may wish to create a tiny fabric sachet to hold the ingredients. Do not hold too close to your nose while inhaling, or breathe over-vigorously. Simply wafting the herbs gently under your nose will do the trick.

Timings
Waxing Moon, Friday, Morning

Find and Gather
» a small piece of fresh Ginger
   root (*Zingiber officinale*)
» 3 drops Peppermint essential oil (*Mentha × piperita*)
» ¼ cup of rock salt
» a mortar and pestle
» a glass jar to store
» a tiny bottle or a small fabric sachet
» artwork of, or book about, someone you admire
» an orange ribbon

The Spell

Place the rock salt into the mortar and pestle.

Grate the Ginger finely until you have about ½ teaspoon and add to the salt.

Drop in the Peppermint essential oil.

While mixing well say:

Awaken my passions

Of book and of brush.

Move blocks in my way,

To inspire my day.

Store in the larger jar, tie the orange ribbon around the neck and leave for seven nights on top of the artwork or the book about the person who inspires you. After seven days, decant the herbs into the smaller bottle or sachet to carry and use as needed.

Alternate Herbs

Any Mint oil can be used in place of Peppermint.

The Pacific Islanders of Dobu chew Ginger and then spit it onto the site of illness to cure it. They also do this towards oncoming storms to keep them at bay.

Peppermint's medicinal use dates back well over 10,000 years, which has earned it the reputation of perhaps being our oldest medicine. It is generally used as a vascular stimulant, disinfectant and an anesthetic.

Burdock and Onion Illness-Absorption Spell

Burdock is a herbal folklore favourite when blood cleansing, purifying and health rejuvenation is sought, making it perfect for a general illness spell. The added properties of Burdock's magickal energies help draw out illnesses and carry them away. Onions are a negative-energy vacuum cleaner and will help boost the power of Burdock in pulling out the illness you are targeting.

Black tourmaline will help protect you while you are opening up to withdraw the illness.

Timings

Waning Moon, Thursday, Midnight

Find and Gather

» 1 teaspoon of dried Burdock (*Arctium lappa*)

» 1 large white onion

» a knife

» a chopping board

» 3 pieces of black tourmaline crystal

» a small red candle

» a small black candle

» a large plate

The Spell

Set the plate near the ill person.

On either side of the plate, place the candles in holders —
the black on the left and the red on the right.

Peel the onion and slice off the top and the bottom so that
it sits flat on the plate and you have a flat area on its top,
then centre it in the middle of the plate.

Place the black tourmaline crystal pieces evenly around
the onion.

Light the candles.

Place the Burdock on the top of the onion, and say:

Draw down to onion,

Draw down and hold.

Illness come here and in onion behold.

A new place to live,

a new place to see.

Leave where you are and to onion now be.

When the candles have burnt down, take all remains of
the spell (except the plate) and onion to a place as far away as
you can manage, and bury. Come back via a confusing path so
that the illness cannot follow you.

Alternate Herbs

You can use a potato in place of the onion, Marigold (*Tagetes*)
in place of Burdock.

Burdock collected
during a Waning
Moon can be made
into a very powerful
amulet to protect
against evil. To make
the amulet, dry the
root and string it onto
a necklace.

Burdock is also used
to cure gout. It can be
eaten as a vegetable,
or its leaves can be
placed in shoes or
bound to suffering
feet.

Yarrow and Calendula Self-Confidence Spell

Yarrow gives courage to those who lack self-confidence. This herb dissipates fears connected with anything that hinders self expression. It also releases negativity. Calendula will actually draw the admiration and respect from others while also helping you realise your potential.

Timings
Full Moon, Wednesday, Midday

Find and Gather

Calendula

» 1 tablespoon of dried Yarrow (*Achillea millefolium*)
» 1 tablespoon of dried Calendula (*Calendula officinalis*)
» a small purple candle
» a candle holder
» 20 drops of Ginger essential oil (*Zingiber officinale*)
» 1 cup of pure water
» a heat-proof glass bowl
» ¼ tablespoon of coconut oil
» a bottle to store

The Spell

Boil the water and pour into the glass bowl.

Stir in the Yarrow and the Calendula, and say:

Herbs of sun, herbs of powers,

I'm leaving you now to brew for some hours.

Set the candle next to the bowl and light it.

Leave the brew to steep until the candle has spent. This will ensure that the energies and attributes of the herbs are imparted into the water.

When ready, strain the water into the bottle and add the coconut oil and Ginger essential oil.

Shake well to mix and, as you do, say:

Confidence, courage, and belief I now know.

Each time my hair is washed,

These things I will grow.

Make sure you shake this shampoo very well each time you use it.

The strained herbs and candle remains can be buried in a sunny section of your garden.

Alternate Herbs

This spell can be made with other herbs, but to remain faithful to the magickal energies you must use at least one of the listed herbs.

The Greek mythological hero, Achilles was dipped head first by his mother, into a bath of Yarrow tea, for protection. Because she held him by his heels, this area of his body was unfortunately unprotected.

Since ancient times Calendula has been strung into garlands to celebrate weddings and religious rituals.

Herb Robert and Ginseng Ultimate-Healing Spell

This spell can support those suffering any illness and injury and help them regain their constitution. Herb Robert has a long association with healing and is highly regarded by the herbal medicine community for the breakthroughs it appears to be making in the treatment of certain cancers and terminal illnesses. In this spell we will be focussing on the powerful energies of this herb to support a return to good health. Ginseng offers endurance so that one can keep their strength in their fight with illness. You must hand-sew this little spell pillow so that you can 'sew in' the healing energy as you go. This spell pillow can be created for someone else, with their permission, or for yourself.

Timings

Full Moon, Thursday, Midday

Find and Gather

- » 1 teaspoon of dried Herb Robert (*Geranium robertianum*)
- » 1 teaspoon of dried Ginseng (*Panax ginseng*)
- » 1 dried organic flower
- » a clear quartz crystal
- » 2 squares of red flannel cloth about 6 x 6"/15 x 15 cm
- » red thread
- » needle

The Spell

Go for a walk and pick the very first non-toxic flower you see. Suitable flowers would be Daisies or Roses. Dry the flower using one of the methods described at the front of this book. Once your flower is completely dry, choose your day to create your spell and make sure you have everything ready.

On one square of cloth place the dried herbs, with your crystal in the centre.

Then lay your flower on top. If your flower is too big, a petal will be enough.

Then say:

Herbs of healing
Crystal of same.
I gift this precious flower –
Please return health again.

Take your fabric with the herbs and crystal and sit in a peaceful and sunlit spot, preferably outside in the garden or somewhere in nature and on the ground. With the red thread and needle, sew the top square to the bottom to seal the sachet. Use whatever stitch you please but make sure that you are focussed on healing and bringing the body, mind and spirit together again with each stitch.

Place the sachet under your pillow.

Alternate Herbs

There are no alternatives for this spell.

Herb Robert is named after the 11th century French Saint Robert Abbot of Molerne, (*1028–1111*). He was known as a very saintly man during his lifetime and one who possessed great medical skills.

Adding Ginseng to chicken soup makes a very tasty and health-giving meal, which is popular throughout Asia.

Rosemary and Jojoba Hair-Growth Spell

This is my personal, secret hair blend and spell which I use with great success to ensure thick, long and healthy hair. If you begin using it the morning after a New Moon and then stop once the Moon is Full, each month, you will encourage your hair to grow long and healthy.

Rosemary is a well-known stimulant for hair growth, as is Cedar. Clary Sage helps balance natural scale oils and is a calmative, which is good if you feel your hair issues are stress-related.

Timings
New Moon, Friday, Midday

Find and Gather

» 4 tablespoons of Jojoba oil (*Simmondsia chinensis*)
» a long, fresh Rosemary sprig in flower, if possible (*Rosmarinus officinalis*)
» 20 drops of Rosemary essential oil (*Rosmarinus officinalis*)
» 10 drops of Clary Sage essential oil (*Salvia sclarea*)
» 5 drops of Cedar essential oil (*Cedrus*)

» 4 tablespoons of coconut oil
» a sterilised glass bottle

The Spell

Wash the Rosemary sprig and hang to dry completely. Once ready, place in the glass storage bottle and fill the bottle with all the other ingredients. Shake well, and say:

Plants of the Earth,
Help my hair grow.
Healthy and long,
With sparkle and glow.

Each night warm about a teaspoon of the mixture in your hands and then massage into your scalp. You will need to sleep with a protective pillowcase or towel dedicated to prevent staining of good bed linen.

Alternate Herbs

There are no alternatives for this spell.

Rosemary has been used since ancient times as a memory booster. Scholars in Greece would wear circlets to help them focus on their study.

Jojoba is native to North America. Native Americans crushed the seeds to produce oils and salves for skin conditions and to soften animal hides. Eating the seeds was also believed to make childbirth easier.

Saffron Happy Healing Spell

Saffron is included in this spell because of its healing abilities and its ability to instill mirth to any atmosphere. This spell would be very good to use when administering care to children or to those who respond well to a lighter attitude. In any case, this handwash will increase the healing powers of spell or magickal work and boost the impact of any type of care given to another.

Timings
Waning Moon, Saturday, Midnight

Find and Gather
- » 1 cup of pure water
- » 1 tablespoon of liquid Soapwort (*Saponaria officinalis*)
- » 3 threads of dried Saffron (*Crocus salvia*)
- » a small frying pan
- » a glass bowl
- » a spoon
- » an empty hand wash dispenser, preferably glass or ceramic

The Spell
Panfry the Saffron for a few minutes over a medium heat, then remove and allow to cool completely.

Pour the water into the bowl and add the Soapwort. Mix by stirring in a clockwise direction, and say:

Healing hands,

Cleansed in flowers.

Happiness return

with health in showers.

Stir three times in an anti-clockwise direction, and say:

Out you go, unhealthy foes.

Take all that is wrong as you go.

Drop the Saffron threads into the mix, one by one, and say with each:

One for healing,

One for mirth,

and one for strength upon this Earth.

Bottle the mix in the handwash dispenser and then use to wash your hands before performing any magickal spells or work involving healing. The handwash can also be used when caring for those who are sick.

Alternate Herbs

There are no alternatives for this spell.

To stop lizards venturing into your home, folklore suggests that you keep fresh Saffron around the house.

Dried Saffron, as we use it, is created from the stigmas of the flowers of the plant. To produce 100 gm of dried Saffron, it requires 60,000 flowers.

Dill and St John's Wort Joyful-Day Spell

Dill will fill you with enthusiasm for the day ahead when used in this magickal salt scrub. It has the added benefit of making you irresistible to others – another way to have a joyful day!

St John's Wort provides a great cure for melancholy. It also dissipates negative thoughts and moods, so will work beautifully with Dill to help you start your day with a positive vibe.

Timings
Full Moon, Friday, Morning

Find and Gather
» 2 tablespoons of fresh or dried Dill (*Anethum graveolens*)
» 2 tablespoons of fresh or dried St John's Wort (*Hypericum perforatum*)
» 5 drops of Orange essential oil
» 6 drops of Lemon essential oil
» 1 cup of sea salt
» approximately ¼ cup of coconut oil
» a glass/crystal bowl
» an airtight glass jar

Plate XVIII.

St. John's Wort. *(Hypericum perforatum.)*

The Spell

Add the salt and dried herbs to the bowl and stir well in a clockwise direction.

Add the essential oils and then gradually add the coconut oil.

Stop when you are happy with the consistency. You may like a wetter or drier mix and so may use more or less of the oil.

Place in the storage jar and then turn three times in an anti-clockwise direction, and say:

Out you go, gloom.

Out you go, darkness.

Out you go, negative thoughts.

Now turn three times in a clockwise direction and say:

In comes sunshine.

In comes happiness.

In comes positive days.

When required:

Stir your mix with a wood spoon before use so the consistency is even.

You can either add a handful to a warm bath and soak, or use as a scrub in the shower.

Alternate Herbs

St John's Wort » Valerian (*Valeriana officinalis*)

Along with being a revered sacred herb, by many cultures, St John's Wort has been scientifically proven to be effective in the treatment of depression.

Dill seeds were once known as 'Meeting House Seeds'. Early settlers would chew them during sermons.

Cacao Physical-Energy Spell

This knot spell helps you maintain your physical energy.
Keep your hemp-string vessel handy for days when you feel your energy slipping. The
Cacao will impart vigour on your spell and will ensure that your own vigour does not
slip away. You will be filling your vessel with the Sun at the beginning of this spell
and can refill it as needed.

Timings
Waxing Moon, Tuesday, Midday

Find and Gather
- » 9 Cacao beans (*Theobroma cacao*)
- » a ceramic/terracotta vessel with lid
- » a length of hemp string, 9" (*or 23 cm*) long

The Spell
Take your ceramic vessel outside and leave in the sun for three hours. Be sure
to move it, if necessary, so that the sun directly fills the inside of your vessel
all of this time.

Add your Cacao to the vessel and then hold it above your head towards the
Sun.

Turn around nine times, clockwise, and say at the end of turning:
Powered by Sun,
The spell has begun.

Vessel of energy,

Mine to take.

Add your Cacao beans and put your hemp string in.

When you wish to use your spell, take out the length of string and make nine knots in it. With each set of three knots, say:

Knot one, energy sealed.

Knot two, refilled with Sun.

Knot three, energy keep.

Carry the string in your pocket to hold your energy fast. To dispose of used knots, burn and say:

Return to fire for another day.

I'll use again in another way.

Alternate Herbs

You can substitute the nine Cacao beans for nine pinches of dried Cacao.

It is from Cacao that chocolate is created and it is perhaps no surprise that its botanical name translates to 'food of the gods'.

The Aztecs used Cacao extensively in foods and drinks, and the beans were also used as a form of currency.

Angelica Return-What-Is-Lost Spell

This spell can be used to return anything at all – from lost keys, to a lost lover or lost pet. If you do not have a tree on your property then find a tree nearby that you feel evokes strength and wisdom. Although this spell works by sending out energies for lost things to be returned to you, it may sometimes provide you with a vision of where your lost thing may be. Angelica is named after the Archangel Michael and while this will boost the spell's powers, especially for those who work with the Angelic Realm, the true power of this plant is its thick and twisting root system. This will pull in and hold the energy of return for you, and ground it.

Timings
New Moon, Monday, Midnight

Find and Gather
» Angelica Root (*Angelica archangelica*)
» red thread
» a tiny piece of paper
» a pen/pencil
» gifts for tree:
» a gold coin
» a tiny piece of cake
» a cup of spring water

The Spell

Draw the thing that you have lost on the paper and then wrap it around the piece of Angelica Root.

Tie the red thread around this bundle leaving a long thread loose.

Take your spell out to a tree, tie it to a branch, and say:

Oh great tree, look far and wide.

Find my treasure and return to my side.

Look inside my petition to you,

And grant my request, oh please do!

Feed the tree with your gifts of a gold coin, a piece of cake and a glass of spring water.

Be sure to repeat this gift-giving when your thing is returned.

Alternate Herbs

There are no alternatives for this spell.

Angelica is native to Syria. Its leaves have a high sugar content and so it is popular in fruit recipes as a processed sugar substitute.

Angelica tea helps heal many conditions, including digestive ailments, and is thought to be a good general-health tonic that supports a healthy circulation as well as providing mental harmony.

Chamomile and Vetiver Fear-Banishing Spell

Creating a selection of candle-anointing oils to keep in your personal apothecary, ahead of time, is good magickal practice.
Chamomile is added to this spell for its calming and soothing properties, which will help those who bask under the light of this candle to hold on until the fears dissipate. Vetiver is a calming addition and helps ground and unify energies, allowing you to think clearly, from a balanced perspective, about your fears.

Timings
Waning Moon, Saturday, Midnight

Find and Gather

» 1 tablespoon of fresh or dried Chamomile (*Chamaemelum nobile*)
» 7 drops of Vetiver essential oil (*Vetiver zizanioides*)
» 4 tablespoons of almond oil
» a strainer
» a glass/crystal bowl
» a glass bottle for storage
» a white candle

Chamomile

The Spell

Place the almond oil into the glass/crystal bowl. Mix in the Chamomile, and say:

> *Fears will come and fears will grow,*
>
> *Flower of calm will face them with grace.*

Drop in the Vetiver essential oil, mixing together, and say:

> *Together we shall stand,*
>
> *and fear shall fall.*

Light the white candle and set it safely in a holder next to the mixture.

Leave to steep for a few hours in a sunlit position.

Strain the mixture into a glass storage bottle and store in a cool, dry place.

Bury the Chamomile plant matter and the candle remains in a sunny spot in the earth.

To use, place a drop of the oil in the centre of a candle and gently massage in. You can use any colour candle, but white is the best because it wards off doubts and fears while also offering protection.

Alternate Herbs

Chamomile can be substituted with Lavender (*Lavandula*).

Chamomile is known as a 'Plant Doctor' because planting it beside another plant that is not doing well will improve the failing plant's health and vigour.

Vetiver is a type of grass, prized for its roots, which have a beautiful sandalwood-type scent that is incredibly long-lasting. In many Asian countries Vetiver is woven into window screens to deter insects. The screens are sprayed with water each day to release the fragrance.

Thurston del.t   Raimbach sculp.t

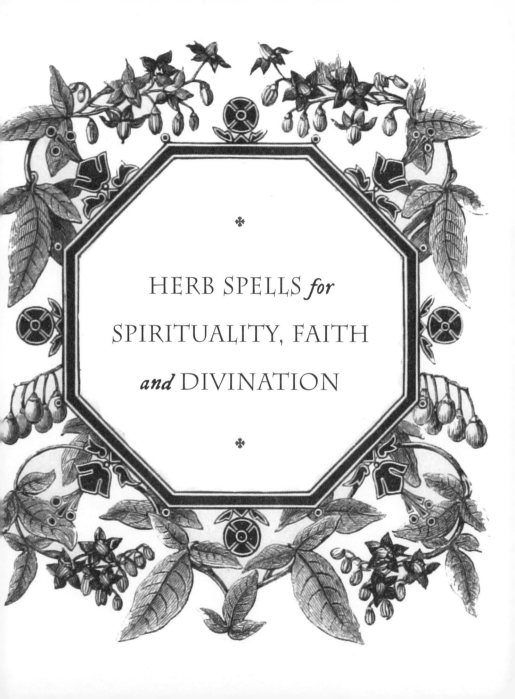

HERB SPELLS *for*

SPIRITUALITY, FAITH

and DIVINATION

Frankincense and Bilberry Mediumship-Improvement Spell

If you are working on your mediumship skills, you will find this incense very helpful. It will enable you to focus your energies more sharply. Included is Frankincense, which works to lift energy, to open up your vision and to offer protection. Most importantly, Frankincense supports spiritual growth. Bilberry ensures clarity, which is valuable when working in this field because it keeps unwanted visitors and entities from visiting you. This incense should never be used to call on those in the spirit world unless you have extensive experience and training in this field.

Timings
New Moon, Monday, Late Night

Find and Gather
» 3 dried Bilberry leaves (*Vaccinium myrtillus*)
» 1 tablespoon of Frankincense resin (*Boswellia*)
» ½ cup of White Rose petals (*Rosa*)
» 2 Gardenia petals (*Gardenia jasminoides*)
» a mortar and pestle
» baking/non-stick paper, and tray
» a glass jar

The Spell

Crush the Frankincense resin using the mortar and pestle.

Add the rest of the ingredients one at a time and macerate each as you combine.

When complete, turn the bowl three times clockwise, and say:

The veil will open and I shall see.

Keep me safe and this side be.

Roll resin into pea-sized balls and lay on baking paper on tray in the sun to dry. Once dry, store in a glass jar and keep in a cool, dry place.

To use, burn as you would any incense, especially during mediumship sessions, to offer protection, clear vision and focus.

Alternate Herbs

The Rose can be substituted for another colour Rose or for more Gardenias.

Bilberry is an important part of the Celtic harvest festival Lammas, or Lughnasadh. At these festivals, the berries are eaten for luck and the branches are used for decoration and protection.

The Ancient Egyptians burnt Frankincense at sunrise in honour of their Sun god Ra.

Evening Primrose Psychic-Energy Replenishment Spell

If you are a divination reader or have had an energetically draining experience, you may like to try this bath spell. Evening Primrose speeds recovery of all types and will also bring you back to your usual state if you have been feeling under the weather. If you are lucky enough to have found, or grown, Evening Primrose flowers, add them to your bath for additional magick infusion. The inclusion of Evening Primrose will also allow your inner beauty to shine.

Sea salt will assist in grounding you while supporting your emotions, and the amethyst crystal helps to focus and replenish your psychic gifts.

Timings
New Moon, Monday, Late Night

Find and Gather

» 4 tablespoons of Evening Primrose oil (*Oenothera biennis*)
» an amethyst crystal
» 2 tablespoons of sea salt
» 2 white candles

The Spell
Set the candles safely on, or very close to, your bath.

Light them, and say:

White light of protection,

Surround me in your grace.

Run your bath, add the Evening Primrose oil, and say:

Heal and glow.

Then add the sea salt, and say:

Ground and balance.

Once the bath is filled to your liking, take your amethyst crystal with you and immerse yourself in the healing and replenishing waters for as long as you like.

Alternate Herbs

None are completely suitable for this spell, although Lavender (*Lavandula*) essential oil (*only use 10–20 drops*) could make a similar bath.

Evening Primrose is native to North America, where Native Americans have used it as a sedative, a painkiller, to heal wounds, for muscle spasms, and as a cough remedy.

Magickal uses for Evening Primrose include its use in spells connected with success and in increasing your desirability to lovers.

Brahmi and Rose Nerve-Calming Spell

This is a beautiful massage and skin oil, which you can use on yourself and on others. Brahmi assists us to remember happy memories and our true inner self while supporting our nervous system and bringing balance. Rose will share love and peace with you.

Use this tonic when you are feeling stressed, nervous or apprehensive.

Timings
Waning Moon, Monday, Midnight

Find and Gather

"SOLITUDE."

» 1 cup of fresh Brahmi (*Bacopa monnieri*)
» 11 drops of Rose essential oil (*Rosa*)
» 1 cup of sweet almond oil or your preferred massage carrier oil
» a clear glass/crystal bowl
» a rose quartz crystal
» a pink scarf or tablecloth
» a large sterilised glass jar
» a beautiful sterilised bottle

The Spell
Wash and completely dry the Brahmi. This could take a day.

In a quiet place, lay out your pink cloth and place your clear glass/crystal bowl upon it. Place the rose quartz crystal inside the bowl and then gently pour your sweet almond oil and Rose oil into the bowl while breathing softly and deeply over the bowl to bring calming energy into the space.

Drop the Brahmi into the bowl, stir in an anti-clockwise direction, and say:

Release, release, release.

Take three deep breaths and then stir clockwise, and say:

Relax, relax, relax.

Pour the oil mixture (without the rose quartz crystal) into the jar and store in a cool dry place for fourteen days. After this time, take out and strain into the beautiful bottle.

Bury the herb matter in your garden.

Alternate Herbs

Rosemary (*Rosmarinus officinalis*) may be substituted for Brahmi. Brahmi oil can be substituted for the fresh plant. Use 2 tablespoons.

Brahmi has been used in India since ancient times as a multi-faceted healing herb. It works well to help with depression, stress, insomnia and fatigue, both physical and mental, while improving memory and concentration.

Roses have a long history dating back to over 35 million years, making them one of our oldest flowering plants. The first cultivators of the Rose were probably the Persians.

Dandelion Divine-Guidance Spell

This is a rather fun spell to create, and it provides a very good way to work out a direction in a matter or to find the answer to a question. Try and keep all your questions and workings with this spell focussed on one issue or area. You will need to do this spell inside, or your Dandelion seeds will blow completely away. Dandelions not only grant wishes, they assist us to see clearly and offer the gift of second sight.

Timings
New Moon, Wednesday, Sunrise

Find and Gather
» 3 Dandelion seed heads (*Taraxacum officinale*)
» a very large sheet of paper or cardboard (*at least A3*)
» pens and pencils
» a glass/crystal bowl

The Spell
Lay out your large sheet of paper and, using your pens/pencils, divide the paper into three sections reflecting the directions/paths you seek. In each section draw something that relates to these directions, even if you don't know outcomes. For example, perhaps you are wondering if you should leave your job and either study or find something else. One section could have a drawing of

the study institution, another a picture of you dressed in your current work uniform, and the third could be a question mark.

Pick all the seeds carefully from the Dandelion and place them into the bowl.

Standing over your paper, close your eyes and start sprinkling the seeds, and say:

Fall where you like, fall where you may.

But show me sweet seeds, my brand new way.

Open your eyes and study the results.

You will be able to find guidance from the seeds via their patterns and the places where they have fallen. Are they all in one section? Are more in one than another? What do the patterns remind you of? See if you can recognise any symbols or shapes in the way the seeds have fallen. If you are unsure of what they may mean, consult a tea-leaf-reading book or online resource for additional insight.

Take photos so you can refer to your patterns later. Take the paper outside, blow the seeds to the wind, and say:

Fall where you like, fall where you may.

Thank you sweet seeds, for your divine insight.

Alternate Herbs

None are suitable for this spell but you can collect and dry Dandelion seed heads for later use. Store in clean dry jars in a cool, dry place.

The common name Dandelion is from the French 'dent de lion' or 'lion's tooth' which refers to the jagged leaves of the plant.

The 'Dandelion Clock' is a popular folklore tradition and childhood game: blow the seed head and the number of breaths it takes you will tell you what time of day it is.

Lemon Balm 'Yes, No, Maybe' Spell

Lemon Balm helps us to reflect deeper on issues we are trying to make decisions about. In this spell you will be creating a type of divination vessel from a bowl of water. This method is usually known as scrying.

Timings
New Moon, Monday, Late Night

Find and Gather
» a handful of Lemon Balm leaves (*Melissa officinalis*)

» a large bowl
» pure water
» a clear quartz crystal
» a black tourmaline crystal
» a smoky quartz crystal
» a beautiful purple cloth
» a green candle
» a blue candle
» a red candle
» a yellow candle

The Spell

Place your purple cloth on a flat surface. This cloth represents 'spirit'.

Rest your bowl on your cloth and half-fill with water.

Place each of your candles around the bowl, to suit your hemisphere/spiritual practice. Usual placement is: Earth – North (green), Fire – South (red), Air – East (yellow), Water – West (blue). You may like to reverse this format to suit the Southern Hemisphere or your geographic location to correspond with the geography of the land. Light your candles. Place your crystal into the centre of the bowl, and say:

Above and Below, from the East and the West,
Herb of vision, now come to rest.
Herbs divine, from below to above,
Help me to see, with truth and with love.

Toss the Lemon Balm leaves into the water and swirl around with your fingers three times in a clockwise direction. Ask your question out loud. Once the water settles, take note of where the majority of the leaves have settled. The crystal they are closest to will be your answer.

Clear Quartz = Yes, Black Tourmaline = No, and Smoky Quartz = Maybe.

Alternate Herbs

None are suitable for this spell but you could try Lemon Blossom flowers (*Citrus × limon*).

Lemon Balm is also widely known as Bee Balm because of the love bees have for the flowers of this special plant.

In 1696, The London Dispensary told its readers that a wine created from Lemon Balm would 'renew youth, strengthen the brain, relieve a languishing nature and prevent baldness'.

Bay Laurel Oracle-Boosting Spell

This bath is very good for those who work with, or who are learning, oracle modalities. It is best used when the moon is Full. Bay Laurel is a plant with powerful oracle energies and protective qualities. Rose water will increase psychic abilities and help facilitate any changes you are seeking.

Timings

Full Moon, Wednesday, Late Night

Find and Gather

- » 9 fresh or dried Bay leaves (*Laurus nobilis*)
- » ½ cup of Rose water
- » 2 cups of sea salt
- » ½ cup of baking powder (*baking soda*)
- » 2 white candles

The Spell

Carve a Full Moon on each candle to help increase your powers.

Set candles safely on or near the bath. Light the candles and say:

Precious light of the Moon,

Shine the way.

Mix together the sea salt and baking powder and add to the running bath water.

Stir in the Rose water.

Float the Bay leaves upon the bath water once it is fully drawn.

Lie in your bath and completely relax.

When you have finished your bath, drain the water and collect all the remains of the spell, including the candle ends, and bury in a dark place on your property.

Alternate Herbs

None are suitable for this spell, although you can substitute the Rose water with Rose essential oil (*10–20 drops*) or a good handful of organic Rose petals.

Bay Laurel was used to create the wreaths that adorned the champions' heads at the very first Olympic Games in 776 BC

The Ancient Romans loved Bay Laurel and would seal letters containing good news with a Bay leaf. They believed that the apparent abundance of the trees was due to them being able to magickally avoid being struck by lightning.

Star Anise and Cinnamon Intuition Spell

This brew will make two mugs of delicious intuition-boosting magick. If you are partaking alone, you can either halve the quantities, to make one mug, and keep the extra in the fridge for the next day, or perhaps come back for seconds!
Star Anise will increase intuition and psychic awareness.

Timings
New Moon, Wednesday, Morning

Find and Gather
- » 1 Star Anise (*Illicium verum*)
- » 1 Cinnamon stick (*Cinnamomum verum*)
- » a fresh pear (*Pyrus*)
- » 1 teaspoon of sugar
- » 2 cups of pure water
- » 2 beautiful mugs
- » additional Star Anise and two Cinnamon sticks

AND THE STAR OF PEACE RETURN.

The Spell
Chop up the pear and place it in a saucepan with some water and the Star Anise and Cinnamon. Bring to the boil and then lower heat. Cover and simmer for another ten minutes. Take off the heat and leave to cool for about fifteen minutes.

Warm the mugs and then strain the mixture into the mugs and add a teaspoon of sugar to each. Place a Cinnamon stick in each and an extra Star Anise.

Stir the brew with the Cinnamon stick in a clockwise direction and say:

Open to knowing

Clear I shall see.

Warmed by the herbs,

So let it be.

Any remains from creating this spell and brew should be buried in your garden or a place close by in nature.

Alternate Herbs

There are no alternatives for this spell.

Star Anise is a herb strongly connected with the New Moon and can be carried with you to bring luck or it can be placed under your pillow to help you dream of another who is far away from you.

Cinnamon raises the vibrations of other herbs it is mixed with. It will also raise psychic powers and open spiritual elements. Cinnamon was a vital essential oil in the Ancient Egyptian embalming process.

Coriander and Wormwood Purpose-and-Path Spell

When working out your purpose, this mist will assist you at every stage. If you ever get lost on the way, just use it again to set yourself back on your path. Coriander will help you to find your hidden talents and skills and will uncover your true purpose. It will calm passionate ideas that may be hindering your true path. Wormwood will support you by showing you deeper possibilities and strengthening your intuition. When the mist runs out, cast the spell again.

Timings
Full Moon, Wednesday, Midday

Find and Gather

» 1 sprig of fresh Coriander (*Coriandrum sativum*)
» 1 sprig of fresh Wormwood (*Artemisia absinthium*)
» a glass/crystal bowl
» 4 cups pure water
» a clear quartz crystal ball
» glycerin
» a large glass bottle
» a small glass misting bottle
» a purple cloth

The Spell
Find a place, preferably outside, where you can leave your essence for an hour

in the sunlight. Place your clear quartz crystal ball into the bowl. Neatly lay out your purple cloth and place your clear glass/crystal bowl upon it.

Slowly pour your pure water into the bowl, and say:

In bright of sun and water pure,

My purpose I seek.

So that in life I am sure.

Put your herbs into the water, one by one. As you place each into the water say (each time):

I welcome sunshine, I welcome happiness, I embrace my purpose.

Leave your essence water and herbs in the sunlight for an hour and then strain into your large bottle. Fill to 4/5 with the water and then top up with the glycerin. Decant what you need into the smaller misting bottle.

Spray into the air in your space each morning (home/work) and repeat the above chant each time. The herbs remaining should be buried in a spot that is always sunlit.

Alternate Herbs

None are suitable for this spell, but if you cannot obtain the preferred fresh herbs then a teaspoon of each, dried, will do. Try to create the master stock when you do have fresh plants, for later use in spells like this one.

Coriander is a favourite in love spells because of its warming qualities. If added to warm wine it will supposedly promote lust in the drinker.

Wormwood is a main ingredient in the drink Absinthe. The herb can be toxic, so care must be taken in all use with it. Hanging it from the rear-view mirror in your car will prevent accidents.

Sage and Nutmeg Faith-Keeping Spell

You will need to find a locket or create one to contain this spell. The locket will remind you of your faith, whether this is simply your personal way of living or a tradition you may follow. Wearing the locket every day will assist you in keeping true to what you believe in.

Sage imparts wisdom, spirituality and faith in this spell, and will help you find your way back to your faith when you feel challenged. Nutmeg, although traditionally thought of as a good-luck charm, warms the soul. It also brings elements and people closer together.

Timings

Full Moon, Sunday, Late Night

Find and Gather

- » 1 teaspoon of dried White Sage (*Salvia apiana*)
- » 1 teaspoon of dried Nutmeg (*Myristica*)
- » ½ cup of sweet almond oil
- » a glass jar
- » very small squares of white flannel (*2×2 cm/½×½"*)
- » a beautiful locket
- » a mortar and pestle

The Spell

Mix together the White Sage and Nutmeg in the mortar and pestle and then pulverise it.

Drizzle in the sweet almond oil and work together in a clockwise direction.

Once these ingredients are well mixed, turn the mortar three times clockwise and say:

The faith I shall keep

No matter the day,

No matter the weather.

Pour into the glass jar and fill with small white flannel squares.

Leave to soak for seven nights.

To use, take out a square, squeeze well and trim to fit your locket.

Use a new square each seven days.

Bury the squares in a sunlit place.

Alternate Herbs

The White Sage can be substituted with any Sage.

A Creole spell includes sprinkling Nutmeg in a woman's left shoe every night at midnight so you can make her crazy with love for you.

The botanical name for White Sage, 'Salvia' comes to us from the Latin 'salvere', which means to heal, preserve or redeem. An Italian proverb relates to us: 'Why should a man die when he has Sage in his garden?'

Sage Blessing Spell

This water can be used any time you would like to bless an object, place or a person. You will be creating it under a Full Moon (the timing is non-negotiable on this one!) Once made, you can use this blessing water at any time and share it with others, so make a nice quantity. If it is raining, collect the water for an added magickal boost.

Timings

Full Moon, Sunday, Late Night

Find and Gather

» Sage (*Salvia officinalis*)

» a mirror

» a cup of Rose water (*Rosa*)

» pure water

» a small handful of salt

» a beautiful white cloth

» a large, beautiful bowl

» a special bottle

The Spell

Find a place outside where you can see the Full Moon.

Lay your white cloth out on the ground and say:

Gently touched with cloth of white,

Ground in Earth for magick tonight.

Set your bowl upon the cloth.

Pour the pure water in and say:

Water of heart, of love and of care,

Support and bring comfort to all that is there.

Pour in the Rose water and say:

Empowered with flowers,

Their love and light.

Sprinkle in the salt and say:

Strengthen and ground,

With all of your powers.

Taking the mirror, angle it so you catch the reflection of the Moon and bounce it into the bowl of water, and say:

Light of the Moon,

Add your blessings tonight.

Leave the bowl out for the night. The next morning, bottle the water. This will be best kept refrigerated but you can add a little glycerin to preserve if you wish.

Alternate Herbs

You may include your favourite herbs in this spell.

The ancient Romans believed that eating Sage would make you immortal, as related in their saying, 'Why should a man die who has sage in his garden?'

Rose water is created by steaming Rose petals, which was a common practice in Ancient Persia.

SECTION THREE

How to Create Your Own Spells

Calendula

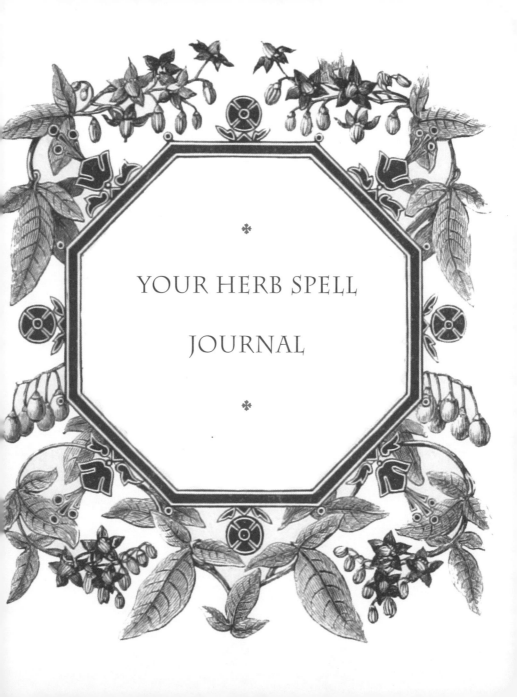

YOUR HERB SPELL

JOURNAL

Title

....

Description

....

....

....

Find and Gather

....

....

....

The Spell

....

....

....

....

....

....

....

....

....

Title

....

Description

....
....
....

Find and Gather

....
....
....

The Spell

....
....
....
....
....
....
....
....

Title

....

Description

....

....

....

Find and Gather

....

....

....

The Spell

....

....

....

....

....

....

....

....

Title

....

Description

....

....

....

Find and Gather

....

....

....

The Spell

....

....

....

....

....

....

....

....

Title

....

Description

....

....

....

Find and Gather

....

....

....

The Spell

....

....

....

....

....

....

....

....

Title

....

Description

....

....

....

Find and Gather

....

....

....

The Spell

....

....

....

....

....

....

....

....

....

Tab. LXXV.

Botanical Meanings

Of course most herbs have flowers, and you can use floral references that explore meanings and uses to develop your own spells. Flowers hold the same energy as the rest of the plant. In fact, they offer an additional boost to the herb's energy because the plant is in the process of reproduction.

Below is a sample of plants featured in this book, but you can find many more in my book *Flowerpaedia, 1,000 flowers and their meanings* (Cheralyn Darcey, Rockpool Publishing, Sydney, Australia, 2017).

Agrimony (*Agrimonia eupatoria*): do not worry, inner fears and worries

Allspice (*Pimenta dioica*): you are worthy, self-value, self-nurture

Angelica (*Angelica archangelica*): inspiration, spiritual protection, facing the unknown, protection

Basil (*Ocimum basilicum*): travel well, open heart, compassion, strengthen faith, spirituality, peace, love, fidelity, virtue, preservation, mourning, courage in difficulties, harmony

Burdock (*Arctium*): do not touch me, protection, healing, persistence, importunity, core issues, release anger

Catnip (*Nepeta cataria*): calm hysteria, clarity, focus, female healing

Chamomile, German (*Matricaria chamomilla*): equilibrium, relax, calm down, release tension, soothing, ease nightmares, energy, patience in adversity, nervous system support, love, attract love

Chamomile, Roman: (*Chamaemelum nobile*): I admire your courage, do not despair, love in austerity, patience, abundance, attract wealth, fortitude, calm

Chicory (*Cichorium intybus*): I love you unconditionally, removal of obstacles, invisibility, momentum, release of tension, favours, frigidity, unconditional love

Chives (*Allium schoenoprasum*): protection from evil spirits, protection of house, weight-loss, protection, long life

Cinnamon (*Cinnamomum verum*): forgiveness of hurt, clairvoyance, creativity, defence, divination, dreams, healing, love, mediation, psychic development, purification, spirituality, success, wealth, power

Cloves (*Eugenia caryophyllata*): protection, dignity, exorcism, love, money

Coltsfoot (*Tussilago farfara*): I am concerned for you, maternal love, concern, children, new challenges, vitality, physical stamina, immunity

Comfrey (*Symphytum officinale*): healing, fusion

Dandelion (*Taraxacum officinale*): I am faithful to you, your wish is granted, long -lasting happiness, healing, intelligence, warmth, power, clarity, survival

Dill (*Anethum graveolens*): lust, luck, protection from evil, finances

Echinacea (*Echinacea purpurea*): higher self, strength, physical strength, immunity, healing, dignity, wholeness, integrity

Foxglove (*Digitalis purpurea*): I believe in you, beware, stateliness, communication, insincerity, magick, confidence, creativity, youth

Frankincense (*Boswellia sacra*): faithful heart, blessing, consecration, courage, divination, energy, exorcism, love, luck, meditation, power, protection, purification, spiritual growth, spirituality, strength, success, visions

Gardenia (*Gardenia jasminoides*): awareness, secret love, divine message

Garlic (*Allium sativum*): good fortune, protection, strength, courage, aphrodisiac, wholeness, immunity

Ginger (*Zingiber officinale*): you are loved, clarity, determination, intelligence, courage, warm feelings, tension-relief, sensitivity, perception, sensory awareness

Ginkgo (*Ginkgo biloba*): beauty, business, calling spirits, dreams, fertility, longevity, love

Ginseng (*Panax*): love, wishes, beauty, protection, lust, grounding, balance, disconnection, longevity, mental powers

Goldenseal (*Hydrastis canadensis*): healing, money

Gotu Kola (*Hydrocotyle asiatica*): self-awareness

Guarana (*Paullinia cupana*): wishes, energy

Hawthorn (*Crataegus monogyna*): balance, duality, purification, sacred union, hope, heart protection

Honeysuckle (*Lonicera*): be happy, I am devoted to you, happiness, sweet disposition, sweet life, end arguments, homesickness, intimacy, unity

Hop (*Humulus lupulus*): apathy, injustice, passion, pride, healing, sleep, mirth

Hyssop (*Hyssopus officinalis*): I forgive you, cleanliness, sacrifice, breath, forgiveness, purification, shame, guilt, pardon, repentance

Juniper (*Juniperus*): journey, protection, anti-theft, love, exorcism, health, healing, cleansing, purifying spaces

Laurel (*Laurus nobilis*): I change but in death, I admire you but cannot love you, victory, protection from disease, protection from witchcraft, merit, glory

Lavender (*Lavandula stoechas*): cleansing, protection, grace, trust, I admire you

Lemon Balm (*Melissa officinalis*): lift spirits, renewed youth, calm, strengthen

mind, restore health, vigour, balance emotions, relax, courage, inner
strength

Lemon Verbena (*Aloysia triphylla*): attractiveness, love, protection from
nightmares, sweet dreams, marriage, purification

Lemongrass (*Cymbopogon citratus*): friendship, lust, psychic awareness,
purification, protection from snakes

Marshmallow (*Althea officinalis*): to cure, humanity, dispel evil spirits, attract
good spirits, beneficence, mother, maternal energies, protection

Meadowsweet (*Filipendula ulmaria*): healing, love, divination, peace, happiness,
protection from evil, balance, harmony

Motherwort (*Leonurus cardiaca*): concealed love, female healing, inner trust,
spiritual healing, astral travel, immortality, longevity, relationship balance,
mothering issues, sedation, calm anxiety

Mugwort (*Artemisia vulgaris*): prophecy, protection, strength, psychic abilities,
prophetic dreams, healing, astral projection, awkwardness, creative
visualisation, visions, clairvoyance, divination

Nettle (*Urtica*): you are cruel, you are spiteful, cruelty, pain, slander, clear
choices, decision-making, protection against evil spirits, health recovery

Onion (*Allium cepa*): protection, purification, detox, hibernation, potential

Oregano (*Origanum vulgare*): joy, happiness, honour

Parsley (*Petroselinum crispum*): entertainment, feast, protection of food, festivity,
to win, useful knowledge

Passionflower (*Passiflora incarnate*): I am pledged to another, belief, passion,
religious superstition, religious work, stability, spiritual balance, higher
consciousness

Patchouli (*Pogostemon cablin*): defence, fertility, releasing, love, wealth, sexual
power

Peppermint (*Mentha x piperita*): friendship, love, clarity, refreshment, concentration, clear thinking, inspiration, energy, alert mind, study support

Scottish Primrose (*Primula scotica*): I love you completely, I'm sorry, compassion, acceptance, anxiety, forgiveness, unconditional love, patience

Red Clover (*Trifolium pratense*): good fortune, good luck, fertility, domestic virtue, protection from danger, psychic protection, cleansing, clear negativity, balance, calmness, clarity, enhance self-awareness

Rosemary (*Rosmarinus officinalis*): I remember you, your presence revives me, psychic awareness, mental strength, accuracy, clarity, remembrance, memory

Sage (*Salvia officinalis*): purification, longevity, good health, long life, wisdom, cleansing, protection, higher purpose, reflection, inner peace, esteem, domestic virtue

Sandalwood (*Santalum album*): clear negativity, mental focus, reincarnation, wishes

Skullcap (*Scutellaria*): relaxation, psychic healing, relaxation of nerves, self-esteem, ability to cope

Slippery Elm (*Ulmus rubra*): stop gossip

Sweet Marjoram (*Origanum majorana*): let go of fear, self-reliance, comforting, relieve physical tension, relieve mental tension, consolation, protection from lightning, comfort grief, fertility, love, joy, honour, good fortune, long life

Thyme (*Thymus vulgaris*): bravery, affection, courage, strength, let's do something, activity

Wormwood (*Artemisia absinthium*): do not be discouraged, absence, authenticity, sorrowful parting

Yarrow (*Achillea millefolium*): friendship, war, elegance, banishing, relaxation

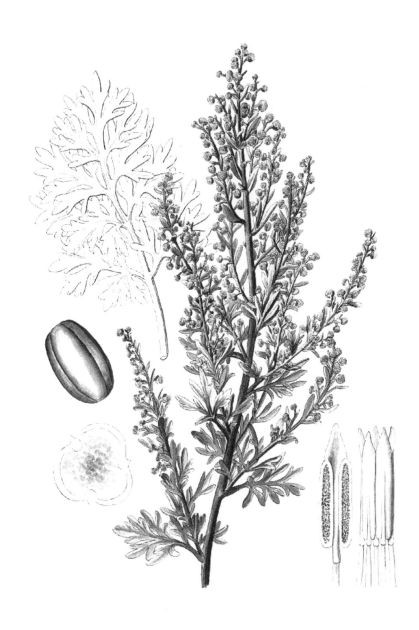

Glossary

basal: arising from the root crown of a plant

bulb: underground stem with modified leaves that contain stored food for plant shoot within

bract: a modified leaf that sometimes looks like a petal

bracteole: leaf-life projections

cardinal points: directions on a compass

cast: to create and release magick

corm: the underground bulb-like part of some plants

corona: a ring of structures that rise like a tube from a flower

compound: a leaf with a division of two or more small leaf-like structures.

cultivar: a plant that has agricultural and/or horticultural uses and whose unique characteristics are reproduced during propagation

cut flower: a flower used as decoration

dominant hand: the hand you are more proficient with using

endemic: native or restricted to a certain place

flower head: a compact mass of flowers forming what appears to be a single flower

floret: one of the small flowers making up a flower head

Full Moon: when the moon is fully visible as a round disc *grounding*: to bring yourself back into the everyday world

hermaphrodite (n): having both male and female reproductive parts

hermaphroditic (adj.): having both male and female reproductive parts.

hex: a spell cast to cause harm

inflorescence: several flowers closely grouped together to form one unit, or the particular arrangement of flowers on a plant

lobe: a rounded or projected part

lanceolate: shaped like a lance, tapering to a point at each end

leaflet: a small leaf or leaf-like part of a compound leaf

leguminous: an erect or climbing bean or pea plant

magick: metaphysical work to bring about change

mojo bag: a magic bag into which magickal items are placed and worn on the person

New Moon: the moon phase when the moon is not visible

oracle: a person who translates divination messages between people and the Other Worlds

ovate: egg-shaped with a broader end at the base

Pagan: originally meaning people who lived in the countryside and now meaning those who follow nature-based spirituality and hold beliefs other than the main religions of the world

perennial: a plant that lives for three or more years

pericarpel: the cup-like structure of a flower on which the petals or stamens sit

pinnate: feather-like

parasitic: gains all or part of its nutritional needs from another living plant

pseudanthium: a flower head consisting of many tiny flowers

raceme: inflorescence in which the main axis of the plant produces a series of flowers on lateral stalks

ray flower: a flower that resembles a petal

ritual: a ceremony that combines actions and sometimes words and music

sessile: attached without a stalk

stamen: the pollen-producing reproductive organ of a flower

staminal column: a structure, in column form, containing the male reproductive organ of a plant

scrying: using a reflective surface or a body of water to gaze into during divination

stem: the main part of a plant, usually rising above the ground

spent: flowers that have died

tepal: a segment in a flower that has no differentiation between petals and sepals

thermogenic: the ability to generate and maintain heat

tuber: a thickened part of an underground stem

Vodoun: a religion created by African ethnic groups in colonial Saint-Domingue and then blended with Christianity in the 16th and 17th centuries

Waxing Moon: when the moon is getting larger, towards Full

Waning Moon: when the moon is getting smaller, towards Dark/New

Tab. 46.

Althæa Dioscoridis, et Plinii. C. B. Pin. 315. — *Althæa Ibiscus.* Dod. Pempt. 655.
Ital. *Maluavisco.* — Gall. *Guimauve ordinaire*

Bibliography

Cook, Will, *Indoor Gardening* (TCK Publishing 2013)

Coombes, Allen J. *Dictionary of Plant Names* (Timber Press 2002)

Cunningham, Scott, *Encyclopedia of Magical Herbs* (Llewellyn Publications 2010)

Graves, Julia, *The Language of Plants* (Lindisfarne Books 2012)

Hall, Dorothy, *The Book of Herbs* (Angus and Robertson 1972)

Hanson, J. Wesley, *Flora's Dial* (Jonathan Allen 1846)

Harrison, Lorraine, *RHS Latin for Gardeners* (Mitchell Beazley 2012)

Hemphill, John & Rosemary, *Myths and Legends of the Garden* (Hodder & Stoughton 1997)

Hill, Lewis and Hill, Nancy, *The Flower Gardener's Bible* (Storey Publishing 2003)

Kelly, Frances, *The Illustrated Language of Flowers* (Viking O'Neil 1992)

Macboy, Stirling, *What Flower Is That?* (Lansdowne Press 2000)

Mac Coitir, Niall, *Irish Wild Plants* (The Collins Press 2008)

Olds, Margaret, *Flora's Plant Names* (Gordon Cheers 2003)

Pavord, Anna, *The Naming of Names, The Search for Order in the World of Plants* (Bloomsbury 2005)

Phillips, Stuart, *An Encyclopaedia of Plants in Myth, Legend, Magic and Lore* (Robert Hale Limited 2012)

Richardson, Fern, *Small-Space Container Gardens* (Timber Press 2012)

Shipard, Isabell, *How Can I Use Herbs In My Daily Life?* (David Stewart 2003)

Telesco, Patricia, *A Floral Grimoire* (Citadel Press 2001)

Thomsen, Michael and Gennat, Hanni, *Phytotherapy Desk Reference* (Global Natural Medicine 2009)

Vickery, Roy, *A Dictionary of Plant-Lore* (Oxford University Press 1995)

Image Credits

Page ii, Hendry, Hamish. Illustration: Woodward, Alice B. *Red Apple and Silver Bells* (Blackie & Son, London, 1897)

Page iv, State Board of Agriculture, Michigan. *Annual report of the Secretary of the State Board of Agriculture of the State of Michigan,* (Lansing, 1862)

Page v, J. Paxton *Magazine of botany and register of flowering plants* (1834)

Page vii, Rose, A. M. *Armand de l'Isle* (Eden, Remington & Co. London 1893)

Page vii, Molesworth, Mrs. *Neighbours* (Hatchards, London, 1889)

Page xi, Hamilton, E., *Flora homoeopathica,* vol. 2- t. (1853)

Page xii, Illustration: Giacomelli, Hector *Songs of the Woods* (T. Nelson & Sons, London 1886)

Page xiv, Dickmann, Jos. F. (firm) *Annual catalogue of Jos. F. Dickmann's reliable garden field and flower seeds* (Jos. F. Dickmann, St. Louis, 1895)

Page xv, Bailey, L. H. *Cyclopedia of American Horticulture* (The Macmillan Company, New York, 1900)

Page xvi, Bulwer, Lytton. Illustrator: Speed, Lancelot. *The Last Days of Pompeii* (Service & Paton, London, 1897)

HERB SPELLS FOR LOVE, ROMANCE AND FRIENDSHIP

In Fairy Land, A series of pictures from the elf-world Doyle, Richard. (Longmans & Co. London, 1870)

Motherwort and Lemon Verbena Dispute Spell
An illustrated flora of the Northern United States Britton, Nathaniel Lord and Brown, Addison (New York : Scribner 1913)

Slippery Elm Release-Anger Spell
Sights in Boston and suburbs, or, Guide to the stranger Pulsifer, David and Andrew, John (John P. Jewett & Co. Jewett, Proctor & Worthington 1856)

Parsley and Mint Attraction Spell
Deutsche Flora. Pharmaceutisch-medicinische Botanik Karsten, H., (J. M. Spaeth, Berlin, 1883)

Comfrey and Dill Get-Closer Spell
The book of the Thames Hall, S. C. (London, 1877)

Damiana and Cardamom New-Lover Spell
Scientific and applied pharmacognosy intended for the use of students in pharmacy Kraemer, Henry (Wiley, New York 1920)

Basil and Red Clover Fidelity Spell
The Works of Francis Bacon Bacon, Francis, Illustrator: Montagu, B. (William Pickering, London, 1825)

Meadowsweet Relationship-Ending Spell
Hardy perennial plants J.T. Lovett Company (Little Silver, N.J. 1907)

Marjoram Communication Spell
Wenceslas Hollar (1607-1677)

Chicory Obstacle-Remover Spell
Annual report of the Secretary of the State Board of Agriculture of the State of Michiganxcc. State Board of Agriculture, Michigan (Lansing, 1862)

Marshmallow and Chamomile Grief-Support Spell
Althaea officinalis Tournefortianum, Bonelli, Giorgio (1783-1816)

HERB SPELLS FOR HOME, FAMILY AND PETS
Homes of our Forefathers in Boston Whitefield, Edwin. (Damrell & Upham, Boston, Mass. 1889)

Skullcap and Oregano Settle Pet Spell
Nordische Fahrten. Skizzen und Studien Baumgartner, Alexander (Freiburg i. B, 1889)

Hop Neighbour-Boundary Spell
Neighbours Molesworth - Mrs (Hatchards, London, 1889)

Ginkgo, Lavender and Sage Family-Blessing Spell
Die Nadelhalzer Tubeuf, Karl, Freiherr von, (Verlag von E. Ulmer, Stuttgart,1897)

Echinacea and Bay Home-Protection Spell
Flora Nederlandsche tuinen Witte, H., (A.J. Wendel 1868)

Chive Garden-Guardian Spell
Paradisi in sole paradisus terrestris Humfrey Lownes and Robert Young (London 1629)

Garlic House-and-Contents Selling Spell
British flowering plants W. F. Kirby. (1906)

Passionflower Sweet-Family Spell
Chambers's encyclopedia W. & R. Chambers, W. & R. (J. B. Lippincott & Company Edinburgh, 1871)

Feverfew and Comfrey Travel Spell
Flore médicale, vol. 4 Chaumeton, F.P.,(1830)

Lemongrass and White Sage Argument-Release Spell
Little Blossom's Reward Johnson, Laura Winthrop (Phillips Sampson, Boston, 1854)

Gotu Kola Dog-Training Spell
Hortus Romanus juxta Systema Tournefortianum Bonelli, Giorgio (1740)

HERB SPELLS FOR STUDY, CAREER AND MONEY
The City of Dreadful Night Kipling, Rudyard (J. S. Ogilvie Publishing Co. New York, 1899)

Hawthorn Work-Harmony Spell
Magazine of botany and register of flowering plants J. Paxton (1834)

Thyme New-Place Spell
Vaughan's Seed Store Vaughan's Seed Company Vaughan's Seed Store, (Chicago, Ill. 1919)

Catnip Change-at-Work Spell
A book of cheerful cats and other animated animals Francis, J. G. (The Century Co. New York, 1903)

Goldenseal New-Skills Spell
Bulletin. 1901-13 United States. Bureau of Plant Industry, Soils, and Agricultural Engineering (Washington Govt. Print. Off, 1913)

Allspice and Patchouli Luck Spell

The natural history of Carolina, Florida, and the Bahama Islands, vol. 1 Catesby, M., (1731)

Ginseng and Guarana Study Spell

Historic Studies in Vaud, Berne and Savoy, etc. (Memoir.) Read, John Meredith (Chatto & Windus, London, 1867)

Elecampane Legal-Success Spell

Cyclopedia of American Horticulture Bailey, L. H. (The Macmillan Company, New York, 1900)

Wild Yam and Potato Money Spell

The World's Inhabitants Bettany, George Thomas (Ward, Lock & Co. London, 1889)

Valerian Make-the-Best-of-Things Spell

British flowering plants Kirby, W. F. (1906)

Sandalwood and Cinnamon Better-Business Spell

The families of flowering plants Pollard, Charles Louis, (The Plant World Co, Washington D.C., 1900)

HERB SPELLS FOR PROTECTION, CLEARING AND BANISHMENT

The Poetical Works of Erasmus Darwin Darwin, Erasmus, (J. Johnson, London 1806)

Agrimony and Coltsfoot Bad-Vibe Clearing Spell

Nursery rhymes (Cornish, Lamport, & Co.New York 1800)

Tansy and Mugwort Protection Spell

Svensk botanik vol. 2 Palmstruch J.W. et al, (1803)

Yerba Mate Barrier-Breaker Spell

La Terra Marinelli, Giovanni, (Milano, 1898)

Foxglove and Dragon's Blood Complete-Protection Spell

Expedição portugueza ao Muatiânvua Dias De Carvalho, Henrique Augusto. (Lisboa, 1890)

Juniper Berry Personal-Boundary Spell

The American instructor Fisher, George, (H. Gaine, New York 1770)

Garlic Psychic-Attack Protection Spell

Eene halve Eeuw Ritter, Pierre Henri - the Elder (Amsterdam, 1898)

Angelica and Honeysuckle Release, Ground and Balance Spell

The British flora medica (London, 1838)

Nettle and Meadowsweet Reverse Negative-Action Spell

Plantae selectae, vol. 8 G.D. Ehret, Trew, C.J., (1771)

Fennel and Cloves Paranormal-Banishment Spell

The Natural History of Man Wood, John George - M.A(George Routledge & Sons, London, 1868)

Hyssop and Honey Purification Spell

When Life is Young Dodge, Mary Elizabeth. Century Co. New York, 1894

HERB SPELLS FOR HEALTH, SELF-CARE AND HAPPINESS

The Poetical Works of Erasmus Darwin Darwin, Erasmus, (J. Johnson, London 1806)

Ginger and Peppermint Creativity-Boost Spell
  The Indian Alps and how we crossed them Mazuchelli, Elizabeth Sarah.
  (London, 1876)

Burdock and Onion Illness-Absorption Spell
  The British flora medica (London, 1838)

Yarrow and Calendula Self-Confidence Spell
  Vaughan's gardening illustrated Vaughan's Seed Company (Vaughan's Seed
  Store, Chicago, Ill, 1921)

Herb Robert and Ginseng Ultimate-Healing Spell
  The British flora medica (London, 1838)

Rosemary and Jojoba Hair-Growth Spell
  Household stories from the collection of the Bros. Grimm Grimm, Jacob; Grimm,
  Wilhelm; Illustrator: Crane, Walter (Macmillan & Co., London, 1922)

Saffron Happy Healing Spell
  The Poetical Works of Lord Byron Byron, George Gordon Byron – Baron
  (Virtue & Co. London, 1878)

Dill and St John's Wort Joyful-Day Spell
  British flowering plants W. F. Kirby. (1906)

Cacao Physical-Energy Spell
  The World at Home Kirby, Mary (London, 1869)

Angelica Return-What-Is-Lost Spell
  The Castles of the Lothians Bell, J. Munro. (Edinburgh, 1893)

Chamomile and Vetiver Fear-Banishing Spell
  The standard cyclopedia of modern agriculture and rural economy Wright, Robert

Patrick (London, The Gresham, London 1908)

HERB SPELLS FOR SPIRITUALITY, FAITH AND DIVINATION

The Poetical Works of Erasmus Darwin Darwin, Erasmus, (J. Johnson, London 1806)

Frankincense and Bilberry Mediumship-Improvement Spell

The Book of Ser Marco Polo Yule, Henry - Sir, K.C.S.I (London, 1875)

Evening Primrose Psychic-Energy Replenishment Spell

A flora of North America Barton, W.P.C., (1821)

Brahmi and Rose Nerve-Calming Spell

Living Statuary Wendlandt, O. J. (Abel Heywood & Son. Manchester, 1896)

Dandelion Divine-Guidance Spell

Flora homoeopathica, vol. 2- t. Hamilton, E., (1853)

Lemon Balm 'Yes, No, Maybe' Spell

Turn over a new leaf and be convinced that W.W. Rawson & Co.'s seeds are true to name Rawson, W.W. (W.W. Rawson & Co. Boston, Mass, 1902)

Bay Laurel Oracle-Boosting Spell

Songs for Little People Gale, Norman Rowland, Illustrator: Stratton, Helen. (Constable & Co. London, 1896)

Star Anise and Cinnamon Intuition Spell

The Blue Poetry Book Lang, Andrew (Longmans & Co. London, 1891)

Coriander and Wormwood Purpose-and-Path Spell

The British flora medica (London, 1838)

Sage and Nutmeg Faith-Keeping Spell

Fragrans' Hout. (Myristicaceae) Bencoolen, Sumatra, for Sir Stamford Raffles.
1824.

Sage Blessing Spell

Notes and observations Kreutzer, William. Grant, Faires & Co. Philadelphia,
1878

YOUR HERB SPELL JOURNAL

Borders

The Nobility of Life
Editor: Valentine, Laura, (London, 1869)

About the author

heralyn Darcey is a botanical explorer, organic gardener, independent natural history scholar, artist, educator and the author of several books and oracle decks of nature magick, folklore, witchcraft and ethnobotanical traditions. Inspired by her pagan family upbringing and her passion for nature and magick, her work focuses on the spiritual, cultural, therapeutic and physical connections between humans and plants.

Her publications include three flower-reading oracle decks which bring the Language of Flowers through the Doctrine of Signatures alive: *The Australian Wildflower Reading Cards, Flower Reading Cards, Flowers of the Night Oracle*. A flower affirmation deck for daily guidance: *Flower Petals*. Two Australian Wildflower mandala style colouring books: *Florasphere Calm* and *Florasphere Inspire*. Her book *Flowerpaedia: 1,000 flowers and their meanings* presents a language translator for the Language of Flowers complete with correspondence lists to find flowers to match sentiments, ritual use and occasions.

For more information, visit www.cheralyndarcey.com

Other books by Cheralyn ...

The Book of Flower Spells

ISBN 978-1-925682-25-0

Beautiful to behold and sacred throughout time, flowers hold powerful nature magick, entwined with the rhythms of the Earth. Includes:

• Sixty sacred flower spells
• Spellcasting and spellcrafting basics
• Magickal gardening
• Dedicated lessons on how to write and cast your own spells
• A personal grimoire journal section

Available from all good bookstores or online at

rockpoolpublishing.co

Spellbound: The Secret Grimoire
Lucy Cavendish

ISBN 978-1-925017-15-1

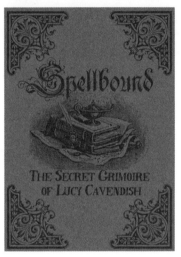

Finally a book of spells to empower you! Spellbound is about connecting you to the magick inside you and activating this transformative power. Come on a mystical journey with Australia's most loved and respected witch, Lucy Cavendish, as she takes you into the secret world of spellcasting. Watch your life become the magickal experience it was always meant to be.

Learn how and why spells work, history of spells, magickal symbols to use in your spells, dressing magickally and the rules of spellcasting.